21 DAYS
of
PRAYER
to
OVERCOME
STRONGHOLDS

21 DAYS
of
PRAYER
to
OVERCOME
STRONGHOLDS

JIM MAXIM
with Daniel Henderson

WHITAKER
HOUSE

Unless otherwise indicated, all Scripture quotations are taken from *The Holy Bible, English Standard Version*, © 2000, 2001, 1995 by Crossway Bibles, a division of Good News Publishers. Used by permission. All rights reserved. Scripture quotations marked (NKJV) are taken from the *New King James Version*, © 1979, 1980, 1982 by Thomas Nelson, Inc. Used by permission. All rights reserved. Scripture quotations marked (KJV) are taken from the King James Version of the Holy Bible. Scripture quotations marked (NASB) are taken from the updated *New American Standard Bible*®, NASB®, © 1960, 1962, 1963, 1968, 1971, 1972, 1973, 1975, 1977, 1995 by The Lockman Foundation. Used by permission. (www.Lockman.org). Scripture quotations marked (NIV) are taken from the *Holy Bible, New International Version*®, NIV®, © 1973, 1978, 1984, 2011 by Biblica, Inc®. Used by permission of Zondervan. All rights reserved worldwide. www.zondervan.com. The "NIV" and "New International Version" are trademarks registered in the United States Patent and Trademark Office by Biblica, Inc. Scripture quotations marked (NLT) are taken from the *Holy Bible, New Living Translation*, © 1996, 2004, 2007. Used by permission of Tyndale House Publishers, Inc., Carol Stream, Illinois 60188. All rights reserved. Scripture quotations marked (AMP) are taken from *The Amplified*® *Bible*, © 2015 by The Lockman Foundation, La Habra, CA. Used by permission. (www.Lockman.org). All rights reserved. Scripture quotations marked (GNT) are taken from the *Good News Translation – Second Edition*, © 1992 by the American Bible Society. Used by permission.

Boldface type in Scripture quotations indicates the authors' emphasis.

21 Days of Prayer to Overcome Strongholds

www.acts413.net
www.strategicrenewal.com

ISBN: 978-1-64123-906-6
eBook ISBN: 978-1-64123-907-3
Printed in the United States of America
© 2022 by Jim Maxim

Whitaker House
1030 Hunt Valley Circle
New Kensington, PA 15068
www.whitakerhouse.com

Library of Congress Control Number: 2022945654

No part of this book may be reproduced or transmitted in any form or by any means, electronic or mechanical—including photocopying, recording, or by any information storage and retrieval system—without permission in writing from the publisher. Please direct your inquiries to permissionseditor@whitakerhouse.com.

2 3 4 5 6 7 8 9 10 11 ⊔⊔ 29 28 27 26 25 24 23

Dedication

I would like to dedicate this book to my closest friend, the Reverend Dr. Herbert H. Lusk II.

Herb and I have walked our journey with Christ together for over twenty-five years, and it has been my privilege. I have never known anyone who knows God "up close and personal" any better than Herb. I have watched him love his family, his church, and the people around him in North Philadelphia and throughout the world. Herb has walked both with powerful leaders and the neediest of people, and he has always remained the man God called him to be—a servant of the Most High God.

I love you, Herb, and I thank you for all you are to me and the example you have shown me of a true man after God's own heart!

Jim

Contents

*From Red Oak
Harla and Rev./
PASTOR
Jan Spring
2024

What would?
Jesus DO?*

Introduction: The Invisible War

*April 28th began.
Key word – Rid set of
procrastination About Private Biz.
Psalms
Corinthians
POWER of GODS will!*

Brothers and sisters in Christ, we are in the middle of a war—a spiritual war raging between two spiritual kingdoms, the kingdom of almighty God and the kingdom of Satan, the god of this world. It is an invisible war taking place all around us. What's at stake? Your success as a Christian, your ability to be productive for the kingdom of God, and your understanding of just how much authority you have as a believer in Jesus Christ.

Your salvation is never in doubt, but your ability to understand the spiritual world, and your ability to be successful against Satan's kingdom, is based upon your knowledge of the Word of God. This book was written to equip you, to give you the knowledge of how to be successful in the spiritual world and how to bring almighty God the glory due His name. You will learn how to pull down demonic strongholds against you, your loved ones, and your friends. This book will help you win souls for Jesus Christ.

We're talking about a real war between good and evil, between opposing forces in the heavenlies. The kingdom of God is one of light, grace, and truth, where Jesus paid the price to give us abundant and eternal life. The kingdom of Satan is one of darkness and offers captivity, destruction, and death. Jesus told us, *"The thief comes only to steal and kill and destroy. I came that they may have life and have it abundantly"* (John 10:10). We cannot afford to ignore this spiritual war.

How do we know that spiritual warfare really exists? Didn't Jesus defeat Satan at the cross? Yes, He did! The apostle Paul gave us the good news:

*For [Jesus] has rescued us from the **dominion** [kingdom] **of darkness** and brought us into the kingdom of the Son he loves, in whom we have redemption, the forgiveness of sins.*

(Colossians 1:13–14 NIV)

So, if we have been rescued from the kingdom of darkness, then why are we still talking about spiritual warfare and the need to overcome strongholds? Because the Bible relates countless examples of this ongoing war. Satan is defeated. Jesus overcame him by His death and resurrection. Yet, the devil is still maliciously at work on this earth. The apostle Peter warned us, *"Be sober-minded; be watchful. Your adversary the devil prowls around like a roaring lion, seeking someone to devour"* (1 Peter 5:8).

Daniel and I have written *21 Days of Prayer to Overcome Strongholds* to accomplish two things:

1. To reveal God-given ways to walk in the Holy Spirit and His Word to overcome *"the dominion of darkness.*

2. To expose the tactics, plots, and deceptions of the devil and his kingdom.

I've been walking with God for over fifty years, and one weakness I've recognized in the body of Christ is a lack of education about the spiritual realm, and along with that, a lack of desire to learn how to use the weapons of our warfare to fight supernatural battles.

Angels, demons, spiritual warfare, warring kingdoms, biblical strongholds—they all exist, but they are not concepts that people consider very often or know much about. Some Christians turn away from even the mention of these words, or worse, roll their eyes thinking, "Oh, no, here we go again." I understand that reaction because some people can be overly emotional about the supernatural. But ignoring this very real hidden war occurring around us or denying the tactics of the enemy of our soul can lead to spiritual captivity.

These next twenty-one days of intercessory prayer will open your eyes to a world that you may have known little about or that confused you because of so much *misinformation* regarding the supernatural. What I can promise you about this short devotional is that by going on this journey with us, you will learn firsthand the truths that dominate the unseen reality of the supernatural world. You will learn the power that almighty God has to free you and your loved ones from Satan's strongholds.

WHAT IS A STRONGHOLD?

*"For the weapons of our warfare are not of the flesh but have divine power **to destroy strongholds**"* (2 Corinthians 10:4). Let's look at some of the words we will be using during our twenty-one-day journey.

Stronghold—a defensive structure; a place dominated by a particular group; a place that is difficult to access or to overcome.

Biblical stronghold—an area of a person's life that functions contrary to God's Word—where Satan holds a person in bondage, and they cannot ever seem to break free.

Intercession—to come in between; the action of intervening on behalf of another.

Biblical intercession—the action of a person who regularly (daily, or even several times a day) goes to God in prayer for themselves or a loved one, continually praying and believing, without reservation, that almighty God can and will break the stronghold that Satan has over them or the person for whom they are interceding.

Demonic—resembling or characteristic of demons or evil spirits; demonic possession or oppression and supernatural activity; weird.

Weird—suggesting something supernatural; uncanny, eerie, unnatural, unearthly.

Biblical explanation of the demonic. In Luke 10:18, Jesus says, *"I saw Satan fall like lightning from heaven."* Jesus said this to reveal the power of God over Satan that exists in the spiritual world. Satan was once the most beautiful and favored angel in heaven until his pride—his desire to be like God—caused him to rebel against the Almighty. As a result, Satan was thrown out of heaven along with a third of the angels, who joined his rebellion. (See Isaiah 14:12–15.)

I can't stress enough that Satan is a defeated foe. Jesus Christ is the King of Kings and Lord of Lords. But the Bible clearly tells us that Satan is still working against us. The devil still seeks to *"steal and kill and destroy"* by capturing believers and nonbelievers alike in sin patterns or behaviors from which they can't seem to escape.

Strongholds from the enemy are not only things like substance addictions to drugs or alcohol; they can also be strongholds of anger, hatred, depression, anxiety, hopelessness, sexual addiction, lust, perversion, pornography, food addiction, gambling, even social media or gaming addictions, and anything else that is dominating a person's life—making them Satan's slave.

Taking this prayer journey together with us will forever change the way you look at the struggles in people's lives. You will gain a greater understanding of the power God has given to all of His children to be used not just for freedom for us, but for the world around us.

Daniel and I know that many Christians are longing to go deeper with God and to break the strongholds Satan has over their lives or the lives of their loved ones and friends. We wrote this book because we want to bless God's people with the truth about the power and authority that we have access to through the Holy Spirit within us. We are so glad to be with you in intercessory prayer during these next twenty-one days.

Remember, at the end of each day, go to www.pray21days.com or www.strategicrenewal.com/21days and join with us as we pray together concerning each devotional day.

God bless you,
Jim Maxim

Join the Interactive
21 Days of Prayer to Overcome Stronghold Experience!

To help you in this prayer journey, go online to access a daily playlist of prayer to be used along with this book.

Here's how it works:

+ Read the devotional for that day.

+ Go online and listen to the corresponding prayers for that day.

+ Pray in agreement with us for the Almighty to help you experience a deeper prayer life for His glory and for your good.

+ Share this resource with your brothers and sisters in Christ that we might all agree together in prayer.

Our hope is that this will be a powerful tool to change your prayer life and help usher you into the daily presence of God.

Visit either of these websites to hear the prayers that correspond with each devotional day:

www.pray21days.com

www.strategicrenewal.com/21days

All Authority in Heaven and on Earth

April

Jim Maxim

And Jesus came and said to them, "All authority in heaven and on earth has been given to me."
—Matthew 28:18

Shortly before He ascended into heaven, Jesus declared to His disciples, *"All authority in heaven and on earth has been given to me."* Jesus was the ultimate victor over Satan and his kingdom through His sacrificial death on the cross and His resurrection. As a result, He was given all authority in heaven and earth from His Father. Jesus wanted to make sure the disciples knew He had won the war, both in heaven and on earth.

Jesus's statement wasn't only for His disciples. He was making a declaration to the demonic kingdom as well. Why? Jesus wanted Satan to know that He had taken all authority back from the demonic kingdom at His death and resurrection. Jesus Christ stripped Satan of his power. Satan is the god of this world but not over us. He has no power over Jesus or over His followers—as long as we remain in Christ and in His Word.

As a result of this authority, Jesus gave His disciples a clear commission to action:

Go therefore *and make disciples of all nations, baptizing them in the name of the Father and of the Son and of the Holy Spirit, teaching them to observe all that I have commanded you. And behold, I am with you always, to the end of the age.*

(Matthew 28:19–20)

Jesus was telling His disciples then and telling us now: "All of the authority has been given to Me, and now I am giving authority to you. Therefore…*get going!* Share My good news. Baptize people into My kingdom. Teach them to observe *all* that I have commanded you. All of it!" God is almighty, and He could accomplish all these things on earth by Himself. But that is not the way He has chosen to work. Instead, God chooses to use us—His children—to work alongside Him. Just like David fought against Goliath to show God's power, the Lord wants us to share in the spiritual battles of this life through the Holy Spirit.

Jesus shares His authority with us only when we are *in Him*, and His Holy Spirit is *in us*. God wants you to be fully aware of the Holy Spirit's power within you. He longs for you to understand the power of prayer and of speaking His Word to overcome the strongholds in your life successfully. That is why, throughout these twenty-one days of intercession, we're going to learn about the tactics of the enemy and the supernatural weapons God has given us to stand against him. Satan doesn't want you to understand anything about your authority as a believer. He doesn't care if you know about this authority in theory. He just doesn't want you to know this truth deep in your spirit. Satan doesn't mind our attempts in the flesh, but he trembles at our confession of Christ's victory over him and the demonic world.

God has rescued us from the kingdom of darkness and transferred us into the kingdom of His dear Son! We are to bear the authority of that kingdom. Let's not waste that authority. Let's learn how to use it in the way God has intended.

THE LORD REBUKE YOU

Even the archangel Michael, when he was disputing with the devil (Satan), and arguing about the body of Moses, did not dare bring an abusive condemnation against him, but [simply] said, "The Lord rebuke you!" (Jude 1:9 AMP)

As we learn about the authority Jesus Christ has given us, we need to understand it in the right context. We have *no authority* in our own flesh. We have nothing to offer anyone except what God gives us. We can't generate the power and strength for battle within ourselves. Jesus was frank when He said, *"Apart from me you can do nothing"* (John 15:5). The apostle Paul wrote, *"I have been crucified with Christ. It is no longer I who live, but Christ who lives in me. And the life I now live in the flesh I live by faith in the Son of God, who loved me and gave himself for me"* (Galatians 2:20).

So, who has the power to ultimately pull down Satan's strongholds over our lives and the lives of our loved ones? *The power is in almighty God alone!* We share it when we call upon His help through His Holy Spirit.

In the book of Jude, the archangel Michael, when battling Satan, simply said, *"The Lord rebuke you!"* No fanfare, no emotional outcry. There is no room in God's kingdom for us to exercise our fleshly strength or our emotions in battle. Our emotions won't produce the results that we're looking for to be set free from the enemy's captivity. It's foolish to try to do it our way! We have to do it God's way.

The power for the battle is in God. The power to rebuke the enemy is in the Lord. Satan must bow to the name of Jesus. So, as we face spiritual battles and seek to overcome the strongholds in life, we will pray, "The Lord rebuke you, Satan," or "The Prince of Peace rebuke you, Satan." We must never forget! The victory is not in our own flesh—it is in the power of God within us!

OUR ROLE IN THE BATTLE

Do we still have a role in fighting spiritual battles over ourselves and our loved ones? Absolutely. Paul tells us, *"Fight the good fight of the faith"* (1 Timothy 6:12).

God has equipped us with powerful weapons for the battle. We're going to exercise our authority in Jesus. We will fight by praising God and spending time in His presence, by humbling ourselves in intercessory prayer before His throne, by standing on God's Word in faith, and by taking up the supernatural weapons of our warfare. The Holy Spirit inside us will give us the power and strength that we need to overcome the enemy of our soul.

Intercession, breaking strongholds, going after the lost and the brokenhearted—it's all God's plan in the first place. Knowing God and knowing that it is God at work in you with His power and His plan enables you to have the victory over demonic strongholds and to destroy them over you or your loved ones.

Let's go to the Lord in prayer together today and ask Him to use us through the power of the Holy Spirit in this spiritual war—to teach us how to fight for ourselves, our loved ones, and our friends. Join us for prayer on Day 1 at www.pray21days.com or www.strategicrenewal.com/21days.

Blessed Be the Lord My Rock

Jim Maxim

*Blessed be the LORD, my rock, who trains my hands for war,
and my fingers for battle; he is my steadfast love and my fortress,
my stronghold and my deliverer,
my shield and he in whom I take refuge.*
—Psalm 144:1–2

Have you come on this twenty-one-day intercessory journey to learn how to overcome spiritual strongholds in wicked places? The first thing we need to understand as we intercede together is *who almighty God is*—the Creator, the Supreme Being, the greatest power that exists in the universe. He is our heavenly Father, our Dad.

THE POWER OF PRAISE

Praise and adoration of almighty God is the foundation of our existence and the key to success in spiritual warfare. Without God as the bedrock of our lives, there would be no reason to consider spiritual warfare. We would be defeated before we even got started. That is why the first principle of spiritual warfare is to know and humbly bless the

Lord God, to say joyfully, along with David in Psalm 144: "Blessed be the Lord, my *Rock*, my *Steadfast Love*, my *Fortress*, my *Deliverer*, my *Shield*, my *Refuge*."

It is so important to get to know our heavenly Father, to spend time in His presence, bowing before Him, confessing His holiness, worshipping Him, honoring Him, magnifying Him. Each morning, I consider it an honor to raise my voice in praise and adoration to God. It is my privilege to come before Him as He invites Himself into our lives. Jesus said, *"If anyone loves me, he will keep my word, and my Father will love him, and we will come to him and make our home with him"* (John 14:23). We are blessed to be able to pursue almighty God—to humble ourselves before Him and confess His glory, power, and omnipotence.

Although we are engaged in spiritual warfare with a hidden enemy, no enemy can ever overcome God's majesty or His kingdom! Yes, God trains our hands for war. Yes, we will learn about the strongholds and tactics of the enemy. Yes, we will wield the spiritual weapons God has given us to overcome him. But first we must understand the importance of being in our Father's presence, *hallowing His name* as Jesus instructed His disciples. *"Our Father in heaven, **hallowed** [reverent and holy] be your name"* (Matthew 6:9).

GOD'S GLORY FILLS THE PLACE

The Bible tells us that praise brings the glory of God into our lives. Second Chronicles 5:13–14 says:

> *(It was the duty of the trumpeters and singers to make themselves heard in unison in praise and thanksgiving to the LORD), and when the song was raised…in praise to the LORD, "For he is good, for his steadfast love endures forever," the house, the house of the LORD, was filled with a cloud, so that the priests could not stand*

*to minister because of the cloud, for **the glory of the LORD** filled the house of God.*

As we praise the Lord, His glory will descend on our lives. So will His pleasure. *"The LORD takes pleasure in those who fear* [reverence] *him, in those who hope in his steadfast love"* (Psalm 147:11). Our heavenly Father will take pleasure in us! That is why this is the first principle of spiritual warfare. To be successful in the spiritual realm, we must honor the Lord God in our mind, in our heart, and in our soul.

KNOW WHO YOU ARE IN CHRIST

We also must know who we are in Christ. I know I'm nothing without Jesus. I can't accomplish anything for Him in my own flesh. But now that I am saved, now that I am washed in Christ's blood, I can declare, "I am a child of God" (see John 1:12); "I am the righteousness of God in Christ Jesus" (see 2 Corinthians 5:21); "I am an heir of God and a joint heir with Christ" (see Romans 8:17); and "I am seated in heavenly places with Christ Jesus" (see Ephesians 2:6).

When interceding in spiritual warfare, I remind myself, "It is not up to me to control spiritual forces. It is up to God as I submit to Him and call upon His name." Jesus Christ lives within me by the Holy Spirit. If Christ lives in me, what's going to come out of my mouth? Christ in me. What's going to be reflected in my intercession for loved ones? Christ in me. Not a single thing is in our own strength and power. That is why I shared this verse earlier: *"It is no longer I who lives, but Christ who lives in me"* (Galatians 2:20). Do you see the difference? That is where the success occurs in spiritual warfare.

Even as we reveal Satan's tactics and deceptions, even as we discuss the weapons of our warfare, our focus will be on the God of our salvation—His strength, His power, His salvation, His Holy Spirit leading and guiding us. It is all about the Father, Son, and Holy Spirit.

Each day I lift my voice in thanksgiving for what the Lord has provided for me. God's plan of salvation has made Satan a defeated foe. Our prayers might sound something like this:

> We worship You, Father. We praise You for who You are, the Sovereign God of the universe, our Creator. We glorify Your name. Father, we acknowledge that we have nothing to offer You. We want to be right before You, Father, always.

> Jesus Christ, we love You. We praise You, Lord. We bless Your holy name. Jesus, You are the King of Kings and the Lord of Lords. Jesus, You're our best friend. Jesus, we thank You today for bringing the Holy Spirit to us.

> Holy Spirit, we yield ourselves to You right now—our minds, our hearts, our spirits. Watch over us. Guide us. Give us wisdom, knowledge, and understanding. Thank You for destroying the plan of Satan against us and our families. Open our hearts and minds to You. Guard us and protect us. Help us to be the men and women You want us to be.

Join us as we pray together on Day 2, and let's experience the power of magnifying the Lord together. Go to either www.pray21days.com or www.strategicrenewal.com/21days.

Day 3

God Didn't Spare His Own Son

Jim Maxim

About the ninth hour Jesus cried out with a loud voice, saying,
"Eli, Eli, lema sabachthani?" that is, "My God, my God, why
have you forsaken me?"
—Matthew 27:46

Have you ever felt like asking, "My God, my God, where are You? Why aren't You answering me? I've been calling out to You for so many years for my husband or wife, my son, my daughter." Have you asked questions like this? Have you seen your life, your loved ones, or your friends' lives overpowered by something that they can't get free from—a demonic stronghold? Have you wondered why God has not done something about it? I'm sure you have. Many of us do at times.

Remember when Jesus cried out to His Father in a similar way from the cross, *"My God, my God, why have you forsaken me?"* He was saying, "God, where are You when I need You the most?"

On the cross, for the first time in history, Jesus Christ questioned His Father. Can you feel the turmoil and despair, the suffering that Jesus felt hanging on that cross? Can you feel the desperation in His voice: *"My God, My God, why have you forsaken me?"* It's hard to imagine why Jesus would ask that question because He already knew the answer. But it is the pain that Jesus as both Son of God and Son of Man had to endure for us.

Today, we're looking to God's Word to show us the answers to this question—*why did God have to forsake His Son?* The Holy Spirit has impressed upon me that unless you know the answers to this question, you will never understand how to destroy demonic strongholds in anyone's life.

WHY DID GOD FORSAKE JESUS ON THE CROSS?

The Bible tells us: "[God] *spared not his own Son, but delivered him up for us all"* (Romans 8:32 KJV).

First—*God spared not His own Son* so that we could have abundant life in Him—in this life and in eternity. The reason for Christ's death is that God wanted to reconcile you to Himself. *"For God so loved the world that he gave his only Son, that whoever believes in him should not perish **but have eternal life"*** (John 3:16).

Second—*God spared not His own Son* so that we, as children of the Most High God, would have the privilege to come before Him in intercession. The sacrifices of Jesus on the cross meant the veil of the temple was torn from the top to the bottom so that we could have access to the Father. *"And Jesus cried out again with a loud voice and yielded up his spirit. And behold, the curtain of the temple was torn in two, from top to bottom"* (Matthew 27:50–51). That is why we can come before the throne in intercession for our loved ones on this journey.

Third—*God spared not His own Son* so that we could have the authority, power, and weapons we need to raise the shield of faith over ourselves and those we are praying for, quenching the darts of the enemy, and pulling down wicked strongholds in their lives. Jesus knew that without the sacrifice of His body on that cross, the demonic strongholds would never be broken. Without Jesus Christ descending into the lower regions of the earth and taking the keys of death and Hades from Satan, we could never have freedom from the domain of darkness. Jesus proclaimed, *"I died, and behold I am alive forevermore, and I have the keys of Death and Hades"* (Revelation 1:18).

> *Therefore it says, "When he [Jesus] ascended on high he led a host of captives, and he gave gifts to men." (In saying, "He ascended," what does it mean but that he had also descended into the lower regions, the earth? He who descended is the one who also ascended far above all the heavens, that he might fill all things.)*
>
> (Ephesians 4:8–10)

What does this actually mean for you and me? We don't know exactly what happened when Jesus descended into the lower regions of the earth. But we do know that Jesus preached to those who were in spiritual prison (see 1 Peter 3:19) and led a host of captives free. He broke the demonic strongholds of hell forever and ever. He took the keys of death and hell from Satan once and for all so that we could live with Him eternally.

So, my friends, the answer to Jesus's question is clear. God forsook Jesus *for us*—so that in your life and in mine, we can go before almighty God's throne because of the sacrifice of His Son. We can lift up the ones who we are crying out for God to set free. We can believe in God's faithfulness because He gave up His own Son for us. In the end, we know that God did not forsake His Son but raised Him up and seated Him at His right hand. By following Jesus Christ, God will not forsake us either.

Now we can say with our understanding: "My God, I know why You didn't spare Your own Son. I understand why Jesus Christ had to die and then descend into the lower regions of the earth. I know that it is the blood of Jesus that gives us our freedom. My God, I thank You for my salvation. I thank You for the death, burial, and resurrection of Your Son to set the captives free. I thank You for the power and authority in the Holy Spirit to pull down strongholds in my life and the lives of my loved ones today!"

Brothers and sisters, be encouraged. Let's pray together today thanking almighty God that He didn't spare His only Son so that we have the privilege to go beyond the veil and into His presence to praise and pray.

Join us for prayer on Day 3 at www.pray21days.com or www.strategicrenewal.com/21days.

Day 4

The Supernatural Majority

Myrids =

Daniel Henderson

Then I looked, and I heard around the throne and the living
creatures and the elders the voice of many angels, numbering
myriads of myriads and thousands of thousands.
—Revelation 5:11

We are in a cosmic spiritual battle. Some aspects of this spiritual battle are clear in the Bible. We are addressing many of them in this twenty-one-day journey. There are other realities we will not understand until eternity. One thing about the battle is very clear—Satan is outnumbered and destined for defeat.

We know that Satan is a "fallen angel." Let's remind ourselves of some basic truths about angels. Then we can learn more about where Satan fits and how he functions in the angelic world. Sadly, most people think of angels as chubby, naked, little creatures with wings on their backs—carrying around a bow and arrows to spread some love. They make for great images on greeting cards and fun home décor, but our common conceptions are full of misconceptions. Contrary to popular belief, we'll never become angels. While angels are actively involved in human interactions, there is no clear biblical evidence that each Christian actually has a personal *guardian angel*. We will be with the angels in eternity when all things in heaven and earth are united in Christ. (See Ephesians 1:10.) We'll gather with them around the throne in glorious worship of almighty God and the Lamb who was slain. (See Revelation 5:6–14, 7:9–12.)

Angels are not omnipresent like God, but they do move very swiftly. Their appearance is often dramatic, like the seraphim around the throne. (See Isaiah 6.) At other times, they appear in more of a human form, even to the point where *"some have entertained angels unawares"* (Hebrews 13:2). Angels are not omniscient, either. They have knowledge of things unknown to us but, as created beings, they are still limited. For example, they cannot read our minds.

We do not know exactly when God created the angels. According to Job 38:4–7, angels watched God work and shouted for joy at the results of the creation, so they were early in the creation story. The Bible describes them as "spirits," "hosts," "sons of God," and "holy ones." The number of angels apparently does not change, as there is no indication that they procreate as humans do. We do not know the exact number, but the apostle John wrote about witnessing a measureless number described as *"myriads of myriads and thousands of thousands"* (Revelation 5:11). Hebrews 12:22 says that when we come to worship, we come into the presence of *"innumerable angels."*

The Bible indicates that angels are organized according to some kind of hierarchy. Michael, for example, is described as the "archangel," and he seems to be a primary leader of the heavenly host. Currently, in this earthly life, we are *"lower than the angels"* (Hebrews 2:7). When Jesus returns, followers of Christ will be raised higher than them. (See 1 Corinthians 6:3.)

The angels' ultimate purpose is to engage in the worship of God in heaven and carry out His purposes on earth, often with extraordinary power. Here's how one writer summarizes their actions:

- They frequently bring God's messages to people. (See Luke 1:11–19; Acts 8:26, 10:3–8, 22, 27:23–24.)

- They carry out some of God's judgments, such as bringing a plague upon Israel (see 2 Samuel 24:16–17) or smiting the leaders of the Assyrian army (see 2 Chronicles 32:21). An angel struck King Herod dead because he did not give God glory. (See Acts 12:23.) They are seen pouring out bowls of God's wrath on the earth. (See Revelation 16:1.) *Thus giving dispay*

- Angels have played an important role in redemptive history, often appearing at significant moments—such as the birth of Christ, the resurrection, and the ascension. *good*

- When Christ returns, angels will come with Him as a great army accompanying their King and Lord. (See Matthew 16:27; Luke 9:26; 2 Thessalonians 1:7.)

- They patrol the earth as God's representatives. (See Zechariah 1:10–11.)

- They carry out war against demonic forces. (See Daniel 10:13; Revelation 12:7–8.) *warriors*

- John records that an angel "*seized the dragon, that ancient serpent, who is the devil and Satan, and bound him for a thousand years, and threw him into the pit*" (Revelation 20:2–3). *not anymore*

- When Christ returns, an archangel will proclaim His coming. (See 1 Thessalonians 4:16; also Revelation 18:1–2, 21, 19:17–18, and other passages.)[1]

1. Wayne Grudem, "Angels in the Bible: What Do We Actually Know About Them?" *Zondervan Academic*, December 13, 2017, zondervanacademic.com/blog/biblical-facts-angels.

Because they are a different kind of being than humans, angels were not corrupted by Adam's fall. They are sinless and holy, perfectly obedient to the Lord's will. But there was a heavenly rebellion that preceded the sin of Adam and Eve, incited by the deceptions of the fallen angel, Satan.

This is where Satan comes in. We know that Satan was a high-ranking angel who led one-third of the angelic host to rebel against God. (See Ephesians 2:2; Revelation 12:1–12.) Since his initial rebellion, Satan has continued to work against God's glorious, good, and gospel purposes in the world in countless ways. We know that Christ will completely defeat Satan in the end, casting him and his demons into the lake of fire. (See Matthew 8:29; 25:41; Revelation 20:10.)

So, what does this have to do with us? As strong as Satan is, we know that he is limited, as already noted about all angels. We know that he is a defeated foe. First John 3:8 tells us, *"The reason the Son of God appeared was to destroy the works of the devil."* Jesus's finished work on the cross pronounced judgment on Satan and destroyed the bondage he seeks to hold over humans as he steals, kills, and destroys. And his forces are outnumbered—*two to one*. Holy angels are twice the number of fallen angels. That's great news!

In our spiritual battle on this earth, we know we are supported by a supernatural majority. God's holy angel *"encamps around those who fear him, and delivers them"* (Psalm 34:7). They guard our ways and *"bear us up."* (See Psalm 91:11–12.) They are sent by God in response to prayer. (See Daniel 10:11; Acts 12:5.) They can be sent to minister and encourage as they did with Jesus, after His wilderness temptation and in the agony of Gethsemane. (See Matthew 4:11; Luke 22:43.)

So, friend, as you overcome strongholds and fight the battles of this life, know that God is on your side and sends His *"mighty ones"*

who still have enough spiritual authority to be called *rulers* and *cosmic powers*. But they don't have more power than the King of Kings!

I don't want to give Satan's kingdom any more recognition than it deserves. Christ has already won the victory over all rule and authority. After Jesus rose from the dead, the Father seated Him at His right hand in heaven, "*far above **all rule and authority and power and dominion**, and above **every name** that is named, not only in this age but also in the one to come*" (Ephesians 1:21). Jesus is already reigning far above all the evil forces of Satan's kingdom! But Satan is still a formidable foe on earth unless we are "*hidden with Christ in God*" (Colossians 3:3).

SATAN HAS NO CLAIM ON JESUS

> *I will no longer talk much with you, for the ruler of this world is coming. He has no claim on me.*   (John 14:30)

When Jesus told His disciples that "*the ruler of this world is coming*," He assured them that Satan had "*no claim*" on Him. Why could Jesus say that? Because He was the sinless Son of God. He had resisted all the temptations and demonic forces that Satan brought against Him. Jesus voluntarily gave up His life on the cross. He defeated Satan and death for all time! "*That through death he might destroy the one who has the power of death, that is, the devil*" (Hebrews 2:14).

So, who does Satan have a claim on? Who can he use his tactics against? Satan can use his tactics on every human being who has ever been born because we were born in Adam's sin. Even Christians who have "been delivered from the domain of darkness and transferred to the kingdom of His beloved Son" (see Colossians 1:13) can't get too cocky. Remember, the apostle Peter warns us, "*Be sober-minded; be watchful. Your adversary the devil prowls around like a roaring lion, seeking someone to devour*" (1 Peter 5:8). Satan's relentless temptations can be destructive even against believers if they do not submit to God and resist the enemy's lies.

Now, we know that Satan can never possess a Christian; our spirits have been born again in Christ. However, he can oppress or influence us with relentless thoughts of depression, anxiety, fear, unbelief, lust, anger, unforgiveness, insecurity, and addictions that can create strongholds in our lives. The darkness that exists in the world today, and the temptations of the enemy, need to be recognized and resisted. Once you open yourself up to Satan's lies and give him permission to come in through your choices, the demonic influence can be very strong. Only God's love and power can break those strongholds.

The spiritual warfare around us is real. But don't let it make you afraid. Fear doesn't come from the Lord. *"For God has not given us a spirit of fear, but of power and of love and of a sound mind"* (2 Timothy 1:7 NKJV). Never forget that almighty God, the Creator of the universe, is stronger than Satan. And the Holy Spirit *living in you* is stronger than the ruler of this world! *"You are of God, little children, and have overcome them, because He who is in you is greater than he who is in the world"* (1 John 4:4 NKJV). God has given us His Holy Spirit to guide us into freedom over the enemy.

Join us on Day 5 as we go before the Lord and thank Him for His Holy Spirit that resides within us and pray for His guidance and wisdom against the wiles of the enemy. Go to either www.pray21days.com or www.strategicrenewal.com/21days.

Day 6

Strongholds of the Mind

Jim Maxim

For the weapons of our warfare are not of the flesh but have
divine power to destroy strongholds. We destroy arguments and
*every lofty opinion raised against the knowledge of God, **and***
take every thought captive to obey Christ.
—2 Corinthians 10:4–5

Have you ever considered that there is a demonic influence that has been assigned against you or your household? Have you ever considered why negative thoughts flood your mind? Recurring thoughts that are so well designed and targeted so perfectly against you. Thoughts that you believed were from you. Thoughts that came out of nowhere that seem so real and too big for you to handle. You just want them to stop; you've had enough! Where are they coming from?

Satan's number one attack is to unleash specific assignments against us, our families, even against our generations. How does Satan accomplish these assignments against us? By speaking negative thoughts and temptations from the pit of hell into our minds in an attempt to build strongholds of sin. Paul calls these thoughts "*arguments and every lofty opinion raised against the knowledge of God.*" He warns us that they must be destroyed.

Ask yourself right now, what is the constant thought or temptation that comes up in your mind? That tries to get you off center from Christ? Is it fear or unbelief? Is it anxiety? Is it lust or sexual perversion? Is it alcohol or drugs? Social media addiction? What is the constant pull against you? Is it negative thoughts that you will never amount to anything? That you are a "loser"? That you'll *never* overcome your addiction, that you'll *always* be like this? In your heart, you can probably name your assignment. It's a reoccurring theme that Satan has designed against you—and he is relentless.

Whoever you are praying for, what is the constant theme in their life? What has them bound by the powers of hell? Is it any of the things we've just listed? Years ago, I realized that Satan's assignment against my family is alcoholism.

I've been ministering to people from all walks of life for decades, and these negative thoughts and feelings happen to nearly everyone I've ever met. From pastors to presidents of companies, from the poor and addicted to some of the wealthiest people on earth, there is a struggle against *these same well-designed strategies* that are targeted against them.

Why are these negative thoughts and assignments so prevalent? Because they are so successful! Satan is predictable. He attacks us with the same obsessive thoughts over and over again. Why are these tactics successful? Because we haven't recognized them as strategies from hell. They are lies from the father of lies. Why would Satan need to change his tactics when he wins against us so often? It is a battle for our minds.

THE GOOD NEWS

The good news is that these negative thoughts can be brought down and defeated because God has given us powerful supernatural weapons. Here is my paraphrase of 2 Corinthians 10:4–5 and what those weapons mean for us:

> The weapons of our warfare are not natural but divine weapons so we can pull down and defeat demonic strongholds and set people free from their power and influence. We can use these weapons *to bring down every negative thought these demonic influences continue to use against people in their minds* and by doing this, their spiritual eyes will be open to see them for what they are, and they will ask Jesus to please set them free.

There is one sure way to defeat demonic thoughts that attack your mind—the authority that Satan will bow down to—and it is the Word of God. We take these negative thoughts *"captive to the obedience of Christ"* by quoting God's Word out loud just as Jesus did when Satan tempted Him in the wilderness. Each time Satan brought a thought, a temptation, or an accusation, Jesus replied with God's Word, *"It is written…"* (See Matthew 4:1–11.) We must do the same.

Satan has been called *"the accuser of our brethren, who accused them before our God day and night"* (Revelation 12:10 NKJV). Often, his condemning words against you are lies about who you are in Christ. Satan's accusations from hell feel so real to us, but the truth is that they are *not true*! Just because the accusations and emotions are powerful *does not make them true*! You bring them down when you say, "The Lord rebuke you, Satan. I stand against these negative thoughts in the name of Jesus Christ. I take these thoughts captive to the obedience of Jesus Christ."

WHAT GOD THINKS OF YOU

What would your life look like if you dwelled on the thoughts that God has toward you and not on those tormenting lies of the enemy? The Bible says we are always on God's mind:

> *For I know the thoughts that I think toward you, says the* LORD, *thoughts of peace and not of evil, to give you a future and a hope.*
> (Jeremiah 29:11 NKJV)

> *How precious also are Your thoughts to me, O God! How great is the sum of them!*   (Psalm 139:17 NKJV)

Satan has thoughts and assignments designed *against* you, but God has thoughts designed *toward* you. What God actually thinks about you is one of the most important truths you will ever learn. God's thoughts toward us and His love for us are revealed in His Word.

There are so many Scriptures we can use to pull down the enemy's lies. When the devil taunts us, we must answer by saying, "I take that thought captive to the obedience of Jesus Christ! God says that He loves me. He has redeemed me. I am His child!" Quote God's Word:

> *I have loved you with an everlasting love; I have drawn you with unfailing kindness.*   (Jeremiah 31:3 NIV)

> *See how great a love the Father has given us, that we would be called children of God.*   (1 John 3:1 NASB)

> *No weapon formed against [me] shall prosper.*
> (Isaiah 54:17 NKJV)

It takes knowing God's Word and using it to speak against Satan's assignments to bring freedom. That's a choice. I am not going to surrender to those negative thoughts, to Satan's assignments of fear and doubt and unbelief! I will not surrender my thought life to Satan. I will honor God by believing and using His Word to resist the enemy of my soul. To be successful in spiritual warfare and in your Christian life, you need to do the same!

Let's go to God together today and ask Him to illuminate our minds and the minds of those we are praying for. Ask that we would understand that God has given us spiritual weapons to take captive any thoughts that are not in agreement with His Word and to pull them down in Jesus's name! Join us in prayer for Day 6 at www.pray21days.com or www.strategicrenewal.com/21days.

Library
any books
of Bishop
'mar mar's' → wow!
teachings   Lobo
life   ‾‾‾
beliefs   wow!

Dressed for the Win

Daniel Henderson

*Put on the whole armor of God, that you may be able to stand
against the schemes of the devil.*
—Ephesians 6:11

It's Super Bowl Sunday. A record-setting crowd has filled the stands. The world is watching via live broadcast. The NFL pros have prepared an entire season for this championship moment. As the teams enter the field, amid the enthusiastic roar of the crowd, one player runs out in a T-shirt, shorts, and flip-flops. He apparently decided he did not need cleats, pads, a helmet, or a team jersey. He just wanted to have fun and be comfortable for the big game.

Ridiculous as this seems, this scene reflects the mindset of too many believers as they enter daily spiritual battle. We are commanded, *"Therefore take up the whole armor of God, that you may be able to withstand in the evil day, and having done all, to stand firm"* (Ephesians 6:13). The message is clear: If we are going to stand firm against the schemes of the devil, resist his onslaught, and live victoriously in the spiritual contest, we must get dressed for battle. Here is our wardrobe for spiritual triumph:

> *Stand therefore, having fastened on the belt of truth, and having put on the breastplate of righteousness, and, as shoes for your feet, having put on the readiness given by the gospel of peace. In all circumstances take up the shield of faith, with which you can extinguish all the flaming darts of the evil one; and take the helmet of salvation, and the sword of the Spirit, which is the word of God, praying at all times in the Spirit, with all prayer and supplication. To that end, keep alert with all perseverance, making supplication for all the saints.* (Ephesians 6:14–18)

As he was inspired by the Holy Spirit to pen this, Paul was probably thinking of Roman soldiers and the armor they wore in battle. But, more importantly, Paul was educated as an expert in the Old Testament, where we discover some powerful related truths about Christ. Our armor is ultimately about the person and provision of Jesus and the truth that our life is hidden in Him. He is our true victor, our strong protector, our sure defense. We are empowered to live in spiritual health and holiness, even in the midst of battle, because of Jesus Christ.

Romans 13:12–14 tells us, *"The night is far gone; the day is at hand. So then let us cast off the works of darkness and **put on the armor of light**. Let us walk properly as in the daytime, not in orgies and drunkenness, not in sexual immorality and sensuality, not in quarreling and jealousy. But **put on the Lord Jesus Christ**, and make no provision for the flesh, to gratify its desires."*

Paul instructed us in Colossians 3:10, *"Put on the new self, which is being renewed in knowledge after the image of its creator."* One commentator clarifies, "Since this 'new man' was the character of Christ reproduced in his people...believers (are) to 'put on' Christ in the sense of manifesting outwardly what they had already experienced inwardly."[2]

Wow! Jesus is completely sufficient to give us victory as we rely on Him, rest in Him, and consciously and daily get dressed in Him. So now, in Ephesians, Paul gives us a more detailed description of our wardrobe for daily spiritual triumph:

"The belt of truth." For a Roman soldier, the belt—more like a girdle—covered the lower abdominal area. This vulnerable area needed protection as it was soft tissue, prone to infection if wounded. This area housed a variety of organs responsible for digestion and the elimination of waste. The belt also covered the reproductive organs.

No doubt, we need truth to protect what comes in and goes out of our life. We need Jesus to protect our relationships and sexual desires. Speaking of the coming Messiah, Isaiah says, *"Righteousness shall be the belt of his waist, and faithfulness the belt of his loins"* (Isaiah 11:5). The Hebrew word here for *faithfulness* is the same Greek equivalent used in Ephesians 6:14 referring to the belt of *truth.* Jesus is our faithful truth that protects vulnerable and vital aspects of our lives.

"The breastplate of righteousness." In Roman times, the soldier's breastplate was typically made of thick leather. It protected him from a fatal injury to the heart and lungs. Referring to our Lord Jesus, Isaiah declared, *"He put on righteousness as a breastplate, and a helmet of salvation on his head"* (Isaiah 59:17). If we are to remain victorious against the strongholds of satanic lies and accusations, we must get dressed by remembering who we are because of Jesus.

Let me remind you again of this truth.

---

2. F. F. Bruce, *Romans: An Introduction and Commentary*, vol. 6, Tyndale New Testament Commentaries (Downers Grove, IL: InterVarsity Press, 1985), 243.

And because of him you are in Christ Jesus, who became to us wisdom from God, righteousness and sanctification and redemption.   (1 Corinthians 1:30)

For our sake he made him to be sin who knew no sin, so that in him we might become the righteousness of God.

(2 Corinthians 5:21)

I *put on* the breastplate of righteousness by affirming with confidence and conviction that when God sees me, He sees the righteousness of Jesus. That is who I am in Him. Each day I can be empowered to *live out* who I actually am—because of Jesus. My heart and very breath are protected in this truth.

Over the years, I've had a reoccurring nightmare. Maybe you've had a similar one. It probably reflects some kind of deep insecurity. I've dreamed that I am at elementary school, and suddenly, I have no clothes on. I might be on the playground or walking home after class. Frantically, I try to cover up or find my clothes. Strange dream—I know.

But, my Christian friend, don't be like a football player wearing beachwear to the big game. Don't be like young Danny in his embarrassing dream. Your greater nightmare is to enter the daily battle to discover that you are not dressed in the armor of Jesus. So, put on Jesus today. He is your confidence and covering!

Before we look at the additional aspects of our armor tomorrow, let's pray together thanking God that He is our truth and our righteousness. Join us for prayer on Day 7 at www.pray21days.com or www.strategicrenewal.com/21days.

Day 8

Head, Shoulders, Knees, and Toes

Daniel Henderson

*He put on righteousness as a breastplate, and a helmet of
salvation on his head.*
—Isaiah 59:17

Stories have been told of a young soldier who encountered his military leader, Alexander the Great. In one account, the soldier's commanders found him sleeping during his watch. Another account says that the young soldier was caught stealing a horse, then brought before Alexander the Great for punishment. In each account, when the young solider was asked his name, he replied, "Alexander, sir." And in both accounts, Alexander the Great became furious and exclaimed, "Young soldier—change your behavior or change your name!"

In our spiritual war, we represent the name of our commander, Jesus Christ. We must then live and fight in a way that honors Him. To do so, we must be battle-ready and wear our uniform—according to His battle plan. So, let's keep getting dressed in the armor given to us in Ephesians 6:14–18.

"The readiness given by the gospel of peace." We've heard that "the shoes make the man." Accordingly, the shoes make the soldier.

Ephesians 6:15 states, *"And, as shoes for your feet, having put on the readiness given by the gospel of peace."* Soldiers must have proper footwear—typically, thick-soled boots that can handle all kinds of terrain and allow the solder to go fast and far when at war.

We are at war and on a mission—a mission marked by *"the gospel of peace."* The supernatural peace of Jesus Christ makes us battle-ready. Isaiah 52:7, referring to the Messiah and His future messengers says, *"How beautiful upon the mountains are the feet of him who brings good news, who publishes peace, who brings good news of happiness, who publishes salvation, who says to Zion, 'Your God reigns.'"* Paul knew this verse well and encourages us to be those messengers today.

We are prepared for battle because, no matter the turmoil and attacks that surround us, we experience the indwelling peace of God. Philippians 4:7 assures us, *"And the peace of God, which surpasses all understanding, will guard your hearts and your minds in Christ Jesus."* Good solders cannot be paralyzed by fear and anxiety. As we trust our Savior daily, we fight the good fight with the assurance of divine peace.

We are prepared for battle because we are heralding the truth of the Prince of Peace. We can never forget that the enemy is seeking *"to steal and kill and destroy"* (John 10:10). Jesus came to give, not the superficial peace that the world offers, but real peace. (See John 14:27.) This world is filled with tribulation, but Jesus has overcome the world and offers supreme peace. (See John 16:32–33.) What a privilege to announce peace to a divided world and to troubled hearts as we go forth in *the shoes of the gospel of peace.*

"The shield of faith." In Paul's day, Roman soldiers carried a shield that, in many cases, was full-body size to protect them from the flaming arrows that were typically launched in war. Made of wood, leather, and sometimes metal, these large shields could even be drenched in water to quench fiery attacks. This helps us understand the context of Paul's

admonition, *"In all circumstances take up the shield of faith, with which you can extinguish all the flaming darts of the evil one"* (Ephesians 6:16). Very often, soldiers would advance side-by-side, creating a wall of protection against the incoming darts as their shields linked together.

I love the promise of Psalm 5:12, *"For you bless the righteous, O LORD; you cover him with favor as with a shield."* Our shield is the reality of faith. When I was in high school, my parents gave me a plaque that read, "It is not the greatness of my faith that moves mountains but my faith in the greatness of God." Our faith springs from the truth of the Word of God (see Romans 10:17) and is focused on God, who is truth. We fix our heart on the reality of who He is and live confidently in the promise of His reward. He rewards us with assurance, endurance, victory in our battles—and so much more.

Like the Roman soldiers, we need one another. We need to link our shields. We do not fight alone. We are part of the body of Christ, a united army. Through intercessory prayer, mutual encouragement, and shared ministry, we fight shoulder-to-shoulder in faith. We can be victorious over the devil's fiery darts of doubt, despair, and defeat.

"The helmet of salvation." Leather helmets, reinforced with metal plates at the forehead and temples, provided vital protection for Roman soldiers. These helmets provided a defense against blows to the head or even a fall from a horse.

Salvation is our helmet. We are protected from the damaging blows of insecurity, confusion, and fear by the assurance of knowing that *"by grace"* we have been saved through faith. And this is not our own doing; *"it is the gift of God"* (Ephesians 2:8).

> *He saved us, not because of works done by us in righteousness, but according to his own mercy, by the washing of regeneration*

*and renewal of the Holy Spirit, whom he poured out on us richly
through Jesus Christ our Savior.* (Titus 3:5–6)

What assurance and confidence! We are confident of His grace that has saved us from the penalty of sin. We trust in His grace that is saving us from the present power of sin. Titus 2:11 assures us, *"For the grace of God has appeared, bringing salvation for all people."* The helmet of salvation gives us power to live in purity and power in this present age. But that is not all. Titus 2:13 continues, *"Waiting for our blessed hope, the appearing of the glory of our great God and Savior Jesus Christ."* Someday soon, we will be saved from the very presence of sin. With real hope and certainty, we fight on in this temporary life, with our minds and thoughts safeguarded by our sure salvation.

Remember, Isaiah 59:17 speaks of our Lord in this way, *"He put on righteousness as a breastplate, and a helmet of salvation on his head."* We are reminded here of His power to deliver His people and defeat His enemies. Thank God that He has placed His helmet of salvation on our heads!

Even though we often falter and fail, our Commander Jesus never declares, "Change your name or change your behavior." Rather, He pledges, "I have given you My name through the grace of salvation, and I will supernaturally change your behavior through the renewing of your mind. Secure your helmet and battle forward in victory!"

Yes, we are prepared for and defended in war—head, shoulders, knees, and toes. Our head is guarded and guided by His salvation. Shoulders to knees, we are covered by the shield of faith. Our toes are secure in the gospel of peace. So, let's fight together in the triumph Christ has provided.

And let's do so now as we pray on Day 8. Join us at www. pray21days.com or www.strategicrenewal.com/21days.

Take Up the Shield of Faith

Jim Maxim

*In all circumstances take up the shield of faith, with which you
can extinguish all the flaming darts of the evil one.*
—Ephesians 6:16

*Now faith is the assurance of things hoped for, the conviction
[evidence] of things not seen.*
—Hebrews 11:1

As we already read, when Paul wrote about the shield of faith, he was probably referring to the well-known Roman shield for battle. The Ephesians knew exactly what Paul meant when he told them, "*In all circumstances take up the shield of faith.*" The Roman soldier would never go to battle without his shield. It would mean certain death. By calling our protection the shield of faith, Paul was letting us know how strong and how powerful faith must be in the believer's life. We can't live our daily lives as followers of Christ without our shield—our faith—either.

Faith is the foundation stone of the Christian life. The Bible says that our faith is the *assurance* of things we hope, the *evidence* of things that we cannot see with our natural eyes. That means that we must call upon almighty God in faith—Someone we *cannot see*—to help us use weapons we *cannot see*—so that we can gain victory in an *unseen world* against an enemy that we *cannot see*. That takes faith! And that is how powerful faith is in the kingdom of God. It is the *evidence* of things in the spiritual *before* we see them in the natural.

We need faith to please God. *"Without faith it is impossible to please Him, for he who comes to God must believe that He is, and that He is a rewarder of those who diligently seek Him"* (Hebrews 11:6 NKJV). We must walk by faith, *"for we walk by faith, not by sight"* (2 Corinthians 5:7); *"stand firm in the faith"* (1 Corinthians 16:13); and even live by faith, *"As it is written: 'The righteous shall live by faith'"* (Romans 1:17).

In spiritual warfare, we also *overcome* by faith, *"For everyone who has been born of God overcomes the world. And this is the victory that has overcome the world—our faith"* (1 John 5:4).

TAKING UP THE SHIELD OF FAITH

How do we use the shield of faith in our battle against the enemy? Paul said that in every circumstance we should *take it up*. This means that we *choose* to lift the shield of faith over ourselves or those we are praying for. We speak the Word in faith, and we pray in faith, believing that God will answer our prayers.

"In every circumstance" means that we choose to do it *daily*. We lift the shield of faith over ourselves first, so that we can be set free to fight for others. The number one thing that Satan uses against Christians is doubt—that relentless doubt that he throws against us every day. The more you take up the shield of faith—faith in God and in His

Word—the more the enemy's cords loosen and the doubts fade. Your mind becomes renewed. In intercessory prayer, we daily lift the shield of faith over ourselves and others. In faith, we speak God's Word over them to protect them and to quench the flaming missiles of doubt, fear, unbelief, temptation, and addiction.

Speaking the Word of God out loud against the enemy's lies encourages our hearts, too. *"Faith comes by hearing, and hearing by the word of God"* (Romans 10:17 NKJV). We need to hear the Word in our spirit daily. We need to discern the attack of the enemy. Speaking the Scriptures over our loved ones quickens faith *within us.* The Holy Spirit uses the Word of God to build up our faith and to open up the eyes of our understanding. Our spirits are awakened; our minds are focused on Him.

When we see a loved one entrenched in the bondage of the enemy, we lift the shield of faith in prayer over them. In answer to our prayers, the Lord breaks the bonds of their captivity. It's not about us. It's about Christ in us. Remember, Paul said, *"Your life is hidden with Christ in God"* (Colossians 3:3).

THERE IS WORK IN EXERCISING OUR FAITH

Do you think that we can go along without experiencing a struggle in the spiritual world? There is work in exercising your faith. That is why Paul tells us to *"be strong in the Lord and in the power of His might"* (Ephesians 6:10). When all of the negative thoughts, accusations, and temptations come against our soul, and our faith is greatly tested, that's where the battle is. We lift our shield of faith by turning to almighty God and exercising the faith He has given us. That is where the victory is. We must become *like a little child* in our faith and *like a warrior* in our fighting! We can pray:

Lord, help us to truly be intercessors, to take up the shield of faith where we can quench all the fiery darts of the wicked one. Help us to resist the power of hell in faith, in word, and in deed.

Let's go to God together with the eyes of faith. Let's raise up the shield of faith over ourselves and the ones we are praying for who are struggling in the enemy's captivity. Let's call out their names before Him, standing against all the demonic lies and deception, quenching all of the flaming arrows of the enemy. Join us for prayer on Day 9 at www.pray21days.com or www.strategicrenewal.com/21days.

Sharper Than
Any Two-Edged Sword

Jim Maxim

*For the word of God is living and active, sharper than any
two-edged sword, piercing to the division of soul and of spirit,
of joints and of marrow, and discerning the thoughts and
intentions of the heart.*
—Hebrews 4:12

God listens to our praise and worship. God hears and moves in answer to our prayers. But Satan only listens to one thing—the living and powerful Word of almighty God. Satan must bow to God's Word. *"The sword of the spirit, which is the word of God"* (Ephesians 6:17) is another piece of our divine armor, a powerful offensive weapon God has given us to overcome spiritual strongholds.

God's Word is not just letters in ink on a page. Hebrews 4:12 tells us that the Word of God is alive! It is *living* and *quick* and *active* and *sharper* than any two-edged sword. It can *pierce* and *divide* between our soul and spirit so that we can perceive the truth. God's Word is also a *discerner* of our actual thoughts. That is why we are here today to speak the Word of God over ourselves and our loved ones.

To stand up to Satan, we need to know who we are in Christ according to the Scriptures. It is only our place in Christ that gives us any authority. In effect, Jesus is saying to us, "You've got to know Me and My Word because those are the only things that Satan is going to bow down to."

I've learned that overcoming strongholds has nothing to do with my natural abilities. It is Christ living in me that gives me the authority to resist Satan's accusations with the two-edged sword of God's Word. We need to believe and be able to declare, "I know who I am! I am the righteousness of God in Christ Jesus. My name is written in the Lamb's Book of Life. I will be in God's presence for eternity. That is who I am, so get your hands off of me, my father, my mother, my husband or wife, my son or daughter, in the name of Jesus. The Lord rebuke you, Satan!"

No matter what you and I are faced with, the Word of God is powerful in overcoming any stronghold in our lives. We are the victor in spiritual warfare. Christ has already won the victory—Jesus Christ *is* the Word of God.

DISCERNER OF THE HEART

God's Word is a discerner of hearts. Is there anything else in the universe that is a discerner of the deepest thoughts and intentions of the heart? Is there anything else in the universe that can break the spiritual bondage over our loved ones? No!

Think about your loved ones in captivity. Is it rational for a man or woman to turn their back on Jesus Christ? Is it rational for a man or woman to be snorting cocaine, or sticking heroin into their veins, or drinking until they fall into a stupor? Is it rational for them to destroy their bodies physically, mentally, or emotionally by continuing to fill their minds with pornography and gambling? Is it rational that a man or woman would want to hurt themselves or those who love them? No, it's not! That is why we need the Word of God, which is alive, to bring deliverance into their lives.

When we wield the sword of the Spirit by confessing God's Word out loud over our loved ones in prayer, it releases the power of the Holy Spirit over their hearts and minds. God will reveal truth and bring clarity to the one you are praying for. With their spiritual eyes opened, they can take a serious look at themselves and ask, "Why am I doing this to myself?"

The Word of God breaks the bondage. It is a discerner of the thoughts and intentions of their heart. Only God's Word can bring someone into the reality of what they are doing to destroy themselves. Confessing God's Word out loud in faith that these are not just words, but alive and powerful truths, puts a smile on God's face. When we confess His Word out loud over our loved ones, we need to understand and have faith that God is working to release them as we pray.

Do you want to see your loved ones set free from strongholds? Do you want to see them set free from the power Satan has over them? Watch God melt the power of Satan over your loved ones when you're confessing God's Word over them!

I've seen the hardest of men break because the Word of God was faithfully spoken over them. I've watched the power of God's Word break the shackles of those bound with alcohol and drugs. I've witnessed it with my own eyes. I've watched God do it. God longs for His people to take our place as worshippers of Him and as faithful children walking in the power of His spoken Word.

God is longing for you to exercise the authority in Him over the demonic presence in your loved one's life. There is nothing in your life—no power of hell coming against you or your loved one—that cannot be destroyed. There is no power that Satan has that will not bow to the spiritual weapon of God's Word.

Years ago, I was a United States Marine. Near the end of basic training, the time arrived that I was waiting for—the day I could go to the rifle range and fire the M14 rifle—one of the most powerful weapons I had ever seen. As I lifted my weapon and fired at the target, I was awestruck by the fearsome firepower in my hands. It made me realize that all of my training had been good, but I needed to go to the next level. Only the correct use of the M14 rifle in my hands would bring the results necessary to defeat an enemy.

That's the way it is with the Word of God. You have to understand the spiritual weapons that God has given you. They are there for your success as a Christian. I know that there is nothing more powerful than the spiritual weapons of almighty God. He wants you to take these weapons and learn to use them correctly for your spiritual freedom and for His glory. That's why you're on this journey with us.

So, let's go to God today as we load up our weapons with the ammunition of His Word and ask Him to teach us how to aim our weapons correctly. Let's ask God to teach us how to fire our weapons to bring Him glory and bring deliverance to our loved ones and our friends. Let's intercede for our loved ones and declare the power of God's Word over them. Join us for prayer on Day 10 at www.pray21days.com or www.strategicrenewal.com/21days.

Day 11

The Most Powerful Force in the Universe

Jim Maxim

Stand therefore…praying at all times in the Spirit, with all prayer and supplication. To that end, keep alert with all perseverance, making supplication for all the saints.
—Ephesians 6:14, 18

The prayer of a righteous person is powerful and effective.
—James 5:16 (NIV)

Prayer is the most powerful force in the universe. Especially when we speak almighty God's Word over our circumstances and back to Him in faith.

Prayer gives you faith for miracles and faith to see God's supernatural power at work. Prayer is the strongest weapon in our spiritual arsenal to set the captives free. We are to be "praying at all times in the Spirit" for the battles and the victories. I know enough; I've seen Satan in action. I would not dare walk on ground that hasn't been prayed over. I have a prayer team who lifts me up in ministry.

Prayer is taking the time to believe almighty God that His power is greater than the enemy. Prayer is entering into our Father's presence with faith to believe that His power is greater than anything in the universe. Prayer is the privilege to believe God for those who can't receive God's truth right now.

Prayer is surrendering our will to His will and exercising something unseen, *faith*, against and over something unseen, *spiritual darkness*, and enforcing Christ's victory on the cross for ourselves or our loved ones. Remember, *"Faith is the substance of things hoped for, the evidence of things **not seen**"* (Hebrews 11:1 NKJV).

FROM THE FIRST DAY

In the book of Daniel, chapter ten, we learn the power of prayer in the middle of spiritual warfare. Daniel had been fasting and praying fervently for twenty-one days about the future of God's people without receiving an answer to his prayers. On the twenty-first day, a messenger angel appeared to Daniel in a vision. The angel's presence was so startling and so powerful that Daniel fell on his face in awe, while his companions fled in fear. The angel urged Daniel to rise and then explained the spiritual battle that had been raging in the heavenlies since the first day that Daniel prayed.

The angel touched Daniel and said to him:

*Do not fear, Daniel, for from **the first day that you set your heart to understand, and to humble yourself before your God, your words were heard**; and I have come because of your words. But the prince of the kingdom of Persia withstood me twenty-one days; and behold, Michael, one of the chief princes, came to help me, for I had been left alone there with the kings of Persia. Now I have come to make you understand what will happen to your* *people in the latter days, for the vision refers to many days yet to come.* (Daniel 10:12–14 NKJV)

Because the *prince of Persia*—a demonic force in the heavenlies who had some authority over that land—was so strong, God sent Michael the archangel to assist in the spiritual battle. Remember, in Satan's hidden kingdom, there are demons, rulers, principalities, and powers that still influence our world. As Daniel prayed and humbled himself before God, this spiritual prince of Persia was standing against the answer to Daniel's prayer. God, who will never be defeated, sent the powerful archangel Michael to overcome this prince of darkness. Michael is called *"the great prince who stands guard over the* [children] *of your people"* (Daniel 12:1 NASB). Michael is a *prince of Israel* in the spiritual realm.

In effect, the angel was saying, "Daniel, from the first day that you prayed, God heard your prayer. I would have been here sooner with your answer, but the spiritual force of the prince of Persia was too strong for me. God sent His most powerful angel, Michael, to help me win the battle." Don't think that this is just an Old Testament *story.* The apostle Paul himself wrote about this kind of spiritual warfare: *"Because we wanted to come to you—I, Paul, again and again—but Satan hindered us"* (1 Thessalonians 2:18).

What does Daniel's account mean for us? First, it reminds us of the powerful impact of our prayers. Praying is serious business in the kingdom of God. Daniel set out to hear from almighty God. We need to take the time to hear from Him as well. Second, it reinforces the awesome truth that God loves us and that He has given us powerful spiritual weapons, like prayer, to overcome the enemy. That is why Paul says so often in his letters to the churches, "Pray for me."

Don't believe the lies of hell that God hasn't been listening to you. God is saying to you today, "From the very first day you prayed, your Father in heaven heard your cry."

No matter how much of a challenge your spiritual battle is right now, because of Jesus's sacrifice for you, we know that God is at work. Just because you haven't had your answer yet, just because you are still in the process of interceding to take back a soul from Satan, God is at work. The Bible tells us that Satan has taken some captive. (See 2 Timothy 2:26.) But through the power of intercessory prayer and God's Word, Satan will have to release them.

What Daniel did in fervent prayer caused the angels in heaven to fight for him. Today, you're learning that because of your faith in intercessory prayer, God is releasing the angels of heaven, the power of heaven, and the power of His Spirit on your behalf. He is releasing that power upon you and the ones you are interceding for. Even though the deliverance may not happen today, the heavenly answer has been set in motion. The cords that bind you or your loved ones are being loosened. As we pray, we need to receive that truth in faith, humbling ourselves before the Lord as Daniel did, praising and worshipping the God of the universe for the answers to our prayers.

Let's join in prayer today, believing that He is listening, believing that His power is real, and believing that He wants to answer us. Today, let's exercise the authority that He has given to us. Join us on Day 11 at www.pray21days.com or www.strategicrenewal.com/21days.

Day 12

Get Ready for Daily Victory

Daniel Henderson

And lead us not into temptation, but deliver us from evil.
—Matthew 6:13

If you were to Google "prayer" or search for a book about prayer online, you would discover an endless range of options. The various approaches and proposed practices of prayer are so diverse (and sometimes quite strange) that you may not be sure where to start or who to trust.

The good news is that Jesus Himself was clear and concise about what His disciples are supposed to do when they pray. In both Matthew 6:9–13 and Luke 11:2–4, Jesus outlined a prayer pattern we know as the *Lord's Prayer*. We are not supposed to simply repeat the words by rote. In fact, the words are not exactly the same in these two gospels. Rather, Jesus wants us to experience the pattern or rhythm that He outlines as we approach the Father.

What we often miss is that, in the original Greek, Jesus's admonition about this pattern is actually a *present imperative*. In other words, He literally commands His followers to *always* pray in this way. It is a matter of obedience. So, this helps us to cut through all of the contemporary confusion to find an experience in prayer that is truly biblical, balanced, and powerful.

When I teach about the Lord's Prayer, I offer four simple movements for aligning our daily prayers with Jesus's command: *reverence, response, requests,* and *readiness.* After we worship (reverence), we align our hearts and surrender our will to His kingdom purposes and His holy will (response). We then bring to Him our needs, which include daily resources and vital relationships (requests). Finally, before concluding our prayer time and heading into the day, we get to anticipate the reality of battle and trust in Him and His Word for our victory (readiness).[3]

In praying according to Jesus's model prayer, we must never neglect the final focus, *"And lead us not into temptation, but deliver us from evil"* (Matthew 6:13). Do you pray with this kind of focus as you wrap up your time with God? Perhaps not. Many do not. But doesn't it make more sense to obey Jesus and pray according to His guidance?

Why is this important, and how can it change our daily navigation through the very real spiritual battle of our lives? What difference would it make if we prayed in the spirit of *"lead us not into temptation, but deliver us from evil"*? What if we prayed this in true faith on a daily basis?

First, this specific prayer for deliverance from *temptation* and *evil* serves as a constant reminder of the very real spiritual battle we face. Satan is relentless in luring us with various temptations and drawing us into evil each and every day. When we pray this way, we are daily

---

3. We teach on this extensively in many of our resources found at www. strategicrenewal.com and on our Strategic Renewal app, available on iTunes and GooglePlay.

aware of the snares that may await us. We can be prepared for battle as we anticipate, identify, and avoid the wiles of the devil.

Second, this prayer fosters daily *recognition* of the futility of self-reliance in this invisible war. This very prayer is a heartfelt expression of our helplessness to fight the temptations and evil by our own puny human powers. On my own, I am no match for the devil and his demons. I cry out daily for God's protection.

Third, it inspires consistent *reassurance* of God's power to overcome anything the enemy throws at us. We trust almighty God to be our protector. We rely on Him to carry us through the day without getting stuck or snared by evil. We trust Him to protect us from any situation that will devastate us. We declare in faith that He will be our refuge, shelter, rock, hiding place, and protector in any situation.

Spiritual warfare occurs daily. But God's greater victory and power for us, in us, and through us also occurs daily. Yes, even moment by moment.

So, obey Jesus daily. Pray as He instructed. Seek His face in worship from His Word before any other focus. Surrender your will to His kingdom concerns and confess as sin anything inconsistent with His will as you respond. Trust Him for your "*daily bread*" and all that represents in the present situation and needs of your life. Pray over your vital relationships to keep them healthy and holy. But, after making these requests, don't get off your knees until you have prayed *the prayer of spiritual readiness*. This is the cry of the heart that knows itself all too well. But it is also the cry of the soul that knows, at the deepest level, that He is our victor!

Join us now as we pray together on Day 12. Go to www.pray21days. com or www.strategicrenewal.com/21days.

Standing in the Gap

Jim Maxim

*I searched for a man among them who would build up a wall and
stand in the gap before Me for the land…but I found no one.*
—Ezekiel 22:30 NASB

*I looked, but there was no one to help, I was appalled that no
one gave support; so my own arm achieved salvation for me.*
—Isaiah 63:5 NIV

I have always been amazed by these verses. I'm amazed that God
searches for His people to stand beside Him: "*I searched for a man* [or
woman] *who could stand in the gap…but I found no one*" and "*I looked, but
there was no one to help, I was appalled.*" God was searching for someone
who would stand in the gap and help to save the land of Israel—and He
was appalled when He found no one to help.

What does it mean to *stand in the gap*? One dictionary explains:
"to expose one's self for the protection of something; to make defense
against any assailing danger; to take the place of a fallen defender or

supporter."[4] Biblically, standing in the gap means interceding for someone who cannot defend themselves against the spiritual dangers that have come against them.

What amazes me is that almighty God would desire someone He created, someone He formed from the dust of the earth—like you and me—to join Him in His fight to break the bonds of evil, that He would seek out a man or woman to stand in the gap for someone else's benefit. It's a beautiful picture of God's heart cry to fellowship with His creation. It reveals how much God longs to use us as a part of His plan. The Almighty is all powerful and yet He still desires that we would stand on His Word and stand in the gap for others.

We realize that in less than one second, God could break the demonic stronghold that Satan has over our loved ones. You might ask, "Well, why doesn't He just do it?"

We have to understand that sometimes those in bondage actually like being there. There is a part of them that enjoys the sin, even though it leads to destruction. It's hard for us to understand why someone would hold on to the lusts of the flesh when it is bringing devastation into their lives. But that is part of the deception and spiritual blindness that comes from the kingdom of darkness.

In their case the god of this world has blinded the minds of the unbelievers, to keep them from seeing the light of the gospel of the glory of Christ, who is the image of God.   (2 Corinthians 4:4)

Who has blinded their minds? Yes, you read it right; Satan has the power to blind people's minds. From what has he blinded them? From the truth of God's love, the light and truth of the gospel that Christ bought our freedom on the cross. As we stand on the Word of God for someone in bondage today, let's pray for their spiritual eyes

4. "To stand in the gap," *Webster's 1913 Dictionary*, www.webster-dictionary.org.

to be opened to the truth. *"I pray that the eyes of your heart may be enlightened in order that you may know the hope to which he has called you"* (Ephesians 1:18 NIV).

Today, God sees His children crying out to Him. We are here today—standing in God's presence and on His Word—to break Satan's hold over our loved ones or friends. We don't want God to be appalled by our lack of faith. We want to honor Him. We want to take Him at His Word. We want to walk in faith.

We can never forget this verse: *"Without faith it is impossible to please him, for whoever would draw near to God must believe that he exists and that he rewards those who seek him"* (Hebrews 11:6). The only reward that we are asking for today is that almighty God will set our loved ones free.

Today, God is motivating you. The Holy Spirit is prompting you. Jesus is drawing you to Himself to intercede for somebody, to ask the Father to do what only He can do to set that person free spiritually. Believing God for someone else means you are the one who is going to pay the price in intercession and spiritual warfare. You are going to be on the front lines. It's not easy to get up early in the morning, to set up "appointments" with God on behalf of someone else, in order to pray *"the effective, fervent prayer of a righteous man* [that] *avails much"* (James 5:16 NKJV). That's why most people don't do it.

God is still searching for a man or a woman to stand in the gap. Today, God has found you. That's why you are here for this twenty-one-day journey. To take the time, to pay the price, to lift up God's holy Word over your loved one—to make a commitment to stand in the gap for those who can't do it for themselves, for those who are bound by the power of Satan.

Let's go to God in prayer knowing that God is just waiting there for us. Let's go to God in prayer together today, realizing that we are going to face the battle, and with the Holy Spirit's help, we are not going to quit. Join us for prayer on Day 13 at www.pray21days.com or www.strategicrenewal.com/21days.

Day 14

The Keys to Intercession

Jim Maxim

*[God's] delight is not in the strength of the horse, nor his
pleasure in the legs of a man, but the LORD takes pleasure in
those who fear him, in those who hope in his steadfast love.*
—Psalm 147:10–11

Victory can be won in spiritual battles. But Psalm 147 tells us it is not by our own personal strength—not by the *"strength of the horse"* or *"the legs of a man"*—but by the strength of the God who takes pleasure in us.

I'm so grateful that my mother was a woman who knew how to win the victory in spiritual battles through the strength of God. She was a woman who knew how to wrestle down the demonic strongholds over her husband and children in prayer—a spiritual warrior who stood in the gap for my life and my soul. Standing on the front lines in battle, and then watching a human soul come alive for Jesus Christ, is the most beautiful experience in the world!

I want to share my personal experience with you in these next two days, the powerful victory over Satan's strongholds that changed my life forever. This is my mother, Isobel Maxim's, story as well as mine.

Here is our testimony:

I was lying in a pool of my own blood. I had over 300 stitches in my face and five tubes going into or coming out of my body, feeding me and draining me. My jawbone was cracked and protruding through my skin—a compound fracture. Under the influence of alcohol, I had had a horrific car accident, spinning off the road and slamming into a tree. I had been thrown through the windshield and then flung back into the car through the broken shards of glass. As I lay in a hospital emergency room in a deep coma that night, my life as I knew it was over.

My mother rushed to the hospital in the middle of the night, fearing the worst, but it wasn't the first time that she had been called on to battle the demons of darkness. My brothers and I had already given her many nights of anguish.

As soon as she walked through those ER doors, my mother knew that it was bad. The doctors told her I was in a coma, and they had no idea if or when I would be coming out of it. They said I might never see again from my left eye because of the amount of embedded glass they were working feverishly to remove. The gash on the top of my skull was so deep that the doctors were concerned about permanent brain damage. In the natural, things were a disaster.

There was no plastic surgeon on call at the hospital that cold December night, so the young ER resident carefully and painfully stitched my face closed the best he could to keep me from bleeding out. The nurses told my mother to go home and get some rest; there was nothing she could do that night. Slowly, she walked out to the parking lot and got back into her car to drive home. Satan, the enemy of her soul, was attacking her unmercifully.

My mother used to tell me, "Jimmy, Satan was so relentless with me that night. 'Isobel, where is your God now? Tell me about this Jesus Christ.'" She could hear the laughter and the mocking of the demonic world. Not out loud but in her spirit. Mocking her for the time she spent in prayer. Mocking her confession of the power of almighty God and that Jesus Christ was her king. She heard every bit of Satan's malicious taunting in her car that night.

As soon as she got home, my mother fell on her knees next to the bed where she had cried out to God so many times before. I used to hear her, and I would think, "My mom is a little bit crazy spending all this time praying." I did not understand that she was pulling the trigger on her supernatural weapons.

That night, Isobel Maxim was crying out to God for me. "Where are You, God?" she asked. "Why, God? Why have You forsaken me and my son? When is this going to end? God, You see my children, You see my husband, caught in the throes of alcoholism."

It was then that my mother discovered the keys to true intercession. It was then that she learned the secrets that changed my life and can change your life forever.

My mother told me that the Holy Spirit came alongside of her right then and spoke to her spirit, "Isobel, that's enough. Isobel, God understands your anguish just like He did when Jesus hung on the cross that day, when He cried, 'My God, My God, why have you forsaken me?' (Matthew 27:46)." God knows how frail we are. God understands.

"Isobel, that's enough," the Holy Spirit repeated. "Begin to praise God now. Begin to worship the Father and magnify Him. Isobel, you know God's presence; you know His Word. You just have to believe it right now. Isobel, let's not insult Him and His power and His holy omnipotence with disbelief."

My mother listened to the Holy Spirit and broke out in praise, worship, and adoration. As she praised, she also began to quote the Scriptures back to God on my behalf. "Lord, You said to 'Call upon me *in the day of trouble; I will deliver you, and you shall glorify me'* (Psalm 50:15). You said, *'Therefore I tell you, whatever you ask in prayer, believe that you have received it, and it will be yours'* (Mark 11:24). Lord, I'm believing Your Word in faith and praising You for Your goodness and mercy!" That night, she discovered that the keys to true intercession were to include *worshipping* God and *speaking out the promises* in His Word *in faith.*

Mom told me later, "Jimmy, as I was worshipping God, I saw a vision of you lying in bed in your coma, with no signs of waking up. Then, I saw God reach His hand down and with His index finger, He touched your left eye. As soon as I saw His finger touch your eye, I knew that almighty God was healing you. I knew that my intercession was touching His heart. I knew in faith that God was giving me the answer to my prayer. At that moment, the deep peace of God fell on me and all around me."

In tomorrow's devotional, I'll share the spiritual victory that occurred in my life because of my mother's intercession and praise.

My brothers and sisters, I pray that you can feel the very presence of God falling upon you right now. I pray that you would reach out to God. Accept by faith that He will deliver your loved one. Accept by faith that God's power is greater than any demonic stronghold. Praise Him for the victory. Speak His Word out loud. These are the secrets of intercession.

Let's begin to magnify and worship the Lord as my mother did for me in believing prayer. Let us pray and praise almighty God as we bring your loved one before the Father. Join us for prayer on Day 14 at www. pray21days.com or www.strategicrenewal.com/21days.

Day 15

Out of Darkness

Jim Maxim

He brought them out of darkness and the shadow of death,
and broke their chains in pieces.
Oh, that men would give thanks to the LORD for His goodness,
and for His wonderful works to the children of men!
—Psalm 107:14–15 NKJV

During the time that my mother was on her knees interceding for me, I was falling through darkness. While still in a coma, I was plunging down a deep tunnel. I put my arms out on both sides as though to grab a railing, anything that would stop my fall. But it was a free fall, and I couldn't stop it. I'm a pretty big guy, six-foot-three, and I could always work my way out of most situations. But not now.

Finally, my fall came to a halt; I was standing in a dark room. I looked over on my left side, and I saw these two black things, two creatures, standing there. I had never seen anything like them before. When I used hallucinogenic drugs in the past, I saw a lot of things that belonged in the demonic world. But this time was different. I'll never forget it. I knew instinctively that these creatures standing so close to me were demons and were there to get me. I didn't know what they were going to do, but I was frightened.

At the same moment that my mother was at home on her knees, praising God, speaking His Word over me, believing in the power and faithfulness of God to move miraculously in my life—it was then that Jesus Christ came to me.

The most startling thing wasn't just seeing Jesus standing there but realizing what He *wasn't* saying to me. Jesus didn't say, "Look at you. Here you are again. You're a fool, Jim Maxim. Why should I help you now? You were profane; you laughed at your mother in prayer; you mocked My people. You wanted nothing to do with Me, with the Holy Spirit, with My Father."

You know, that's what I would have said to somebody if the situations were reversed. But Jesus didn't say any of that. In fact, when Jesus came to me, I noticed right away that the two demons beside me froze in their tracks. They knew exactly who He was and what He could do *to* them and *for* me.

Jesus didn't even look at them. His eyes were riveted on me. Jesus spoke to me in my heart more than in words out loud. It was like a liquid sea of love. I understood what He was saying. This was my impression of His words: "Jim, you've been playing around long enough. Do you want to continue?" Loving, kind, gentle words. I looked at Him and said, "No, Jesus, I don't. Jesus, what do I have to do?"

I had already prayed a "jailhouse prayer" once when I faced a short prison sentence. But as soon as I was released, I went right back to my bad ways. I repeated, "Jesus, here I am again. What do I have to do?" I couldn't shake the alcohol. I couldn't shake the drugs. I needed intervention. I needed someone to cut the cords that Satan had wrapped around my soul. I needed intercession—somebody to help me since I couldn't help myself.

As my mother was interceding, pulling down the demonic strongholds in prayer and praise, Jesus looked at me and said, "Jimmy, if you ask Me to cleanse you and forgive you, I will. If you ask Me to help you, I'll give you the power to overcome the drugs and alcohol. And I'll never leave you or forsake you, Jim. I will walk with you all the days of your life, and I will be your friend."

I have called you friends, for everything that I learned from my Father I have made known to you. (John 15:15 NIV)

I looked back at Him and said, "Jesus, help me. Please, Jesus, help me." The moment I asked for His help, those two black creatures, those two demons—whatever they were and wherever they came from—vanished.

A couple of days later, I woke up from my coma in the intensive care unit. My mother, sitting beside me, told me about the accident and the 300 stitches in my face. My head was wrapped up like a mummy from the top of my skull all the way down to the bottom of my neck. I still had five tubes in my body feeding me and draining me. I couldn't talk; my jaw was wired shut. Painfully, I muttered my first words through that broken jaw, "Mom, Jesus is here. Mom, Jesus is here." And my mother knew that almighty God had touched me.

Months later, as I healed, Mom used to stretch out her index finger in front of me and say, "Jimmy, I knew it. When I saw Jesus touch your left eye with His finger, when I was crying out for you, I knew that God heard my cry."

From the first day I came out of that coma, I knew that my life was changed forever. I knew that I would never go back to the drugs and alcohol—the evil strongholds in my life that I had permitted Satan to build through my lifestyle and choices. I knew that Jesus Christ was real. That was over fifty years ago, and I have never returned to that lifestyle or that spiritual bondage. *"Therefore if the Son makes you free, you shall be free indeed"* (John 8:36 NKJV).

My life was changed forever because I had a mother who understood the power of prayer in Jesus to pull down demonic forces in my life. What would have happened if my mother hadn't answered God's call to stand in the gap for me? Would I still be enslaved to the bondage of drugs and alcohol? I don't know. But I do know that I can never thank God enough for giving me someone who was a fierce spiritual warrior and battled for my life and my soul.[5]

You are here today, just like my mother, to cry out to almighty God in faith, to worship Him and praise Him, to take up your weapons and see Him break the demonic strongholds over your life or the life of someone you love. You're here today to commit your spirit or the spirit of another into God's loving hands. Let's go to almighty God together in faith and true intercession today. Join us for prayer on Day 15 at www.pray21days.com or www.strategicrenewal.com/21days.

---

5. If you want to read more, my full testimony can be found in my book *Face-to-Face with God: A True Story of Rebellion and Restoration* (Whitaker House, 2011).

Run with Perseverance

Jim Maxim

And let us run with perseverance the race marked out for us,
fixing our eyes on Jesus, the pioneer and perfecter of faith.
—Hebrews 12:1–2 NIV

Let's not become discouraged in doing good, for in due time we
will reap, if we do not become weary.
—Galatians 6:9 NASB

"*et us run with **perseverance**.*" The Oxford online dictionary defines perseverance as "the quality of continuing to try to achieve a particular aim despite difficulties."[6]

To me, perseverance and persistence mean not giving up, but also they mean *taking time*. How are we going to live an abundant life in Christ and be spiritual overcomers if we don't take the time?

Many Christians are spiritually weak because they don't take the time to minister to God. They think that a quick ten minutes of prayer

---

6. "Definition of perseverance noun," *Oxford Advanced Learner's Dictionary*, www. oxfordlearnersdictionaries.com/us/definition/english/perseverance?q=perseverance.

is enough to overcome demonic strongholds against an enemy who spends his time seeking the weak to devour. We need time to get to know God, time to worship Him, time to minister to Him, time to glorify Him. Why? Because He is worthy, and it pleases Him. Almighty God is pleased when we take the time to come to Him and then intercede for deliverance on behalf of someone in desperate need of freedom.

I understand that prayer for someone's deliverance from a stronghold is one of the hardest things we do. The greatest challenge in the Christian life is to show up every day. Standing in the gap for those in bondage is one of the hardest jobs in the world.

Praise God, many times I have experienced the joy and thanksgiving that result when persevering prayers come to pass! I can rejoice with a loved one, a friend, or even a friend of a friend who has been set free!

I also know what it is to stand in intercession for someone for years and face discouragement as I continue to serve God until I see the breakthrough. I have held people in my arms who were shaking and crying out from drug addiction. I've held the loved ones of alcoholics as they watched their loved one die from the clutches of addiction. I've seen firsthand the devastation of someone's life being controlled by forces outside of themselves. Yes, they made the choice to participate in the substances that eventually took control of their lives. No, nobody is forced to let this happen. No, the devil didn't make them do it; it was a choice. But God is still there in His love, mercy, and power to free them from the clutches of spiritual darkness. And He is still calling us to stand in the gap in prayer to battle for the strongholds to be overcome in their lives. If you show up to worship God, He will meet you there. Even when discouragement threatens, God has never left me alone.

If you want to be a soldier of the cross, then you have to pick up your weapons and be willing to fight. If you don't, then the war that you are in will continue to pull you down. Spiritual warfare is just that—it is warfare. Sometimes the weariness is real. Your thoughts are scattered; your emotions are attacked. But God will be faithful to refresh you in His Spirit and His Word if you come to Him in faith, if you come to Him and worship.

That brings me back to the question of time. How are you going to have that kind of faith come alive in your heart if you don't spend time in His presence and in His Word? How will you know the Word if you don't spend time in it? How will you know God if you don't spend time with Him?

I need God's presence to activate my faith. I do that by accepting His invitation to spend time with Him every day. The truth is that if almighty God didn't equip me daily while I am in His presence, I couldn't serve Him. The desire of my heart to intercede for others, and to teach others to pray and speak the Word over those in captivity, comes from God. In that still, small voice, He says to me, "Come on, Jim, I see what heartache you have because of your loved one. I see what problems you have in the business. I've got it solved for you if you're willing to spend time with Me."

ENCOURAGE ONE ANOTHER DAILY

But encourage one another daily, as long as it is called "Today," so that none of you may be hardened by sin's deceitfulness.
(Hebrews 3:13 NIV)

And let's consider how to encourage one another in love and good deeds, not abandoning our own meeting together, as is the habit of some people, but encouraging one another; and all the more as you see the day drawing near.   (Hebrews 10:24–25 NASB)

Fear, doubt, and unbelief are favorite attacks of the enemy against all of us. When we minister to pastors across the country, that is the number-one thing that comes against them. Satan tries to tell them they're not doing anything for Christ, they have nothing to offer anyone, and their ministry is not accomplishing anything. I know that many people think that pastors don't get discouraged. This couldn't be further from the truth. Discouragement is the biggest thing that Satan uses against those in ministry.

Is that what he is using against you as you press into God and His Word during these twenty-one days? There is nothing Satan won't do to try to discourage us. The way we fight discouragement is revealed in God's Word. The Bible tells us to renew our minds daily, to seek God in prayer daily, to put on the armor daily, to hold the shield of faith daily—*and to encourage one another daily while it is still called Today*!

Right now, we are going to stand on the front line of battle for our loved ones. We are going to pray, "Father, I'm here because You told me to come. You told me to ask and keep on asking. You told me to persevere. You told me to intercede. You told me to cry out to You—to stand in the gap, do my part, and stand in Your glory and Your power." Join us for prayer on Day 16 at www.pray21days.com or www.strategicrenewal.com/21days.

Is God Enough for You?

Jim Maxim

*Satan rose up against Israel and caused [incited] David to take
a census of the people of Israel.*
—1 Chronicles 21:1 NLT

In God is everything we need. God needs to be enough for us. Is God enough for you?

In the Old Testament, David was a man "after God's own heart." (See 1 Samuel 13:14.) Yet, every time David decided that God wasn't enough for him, Satan set up a trap. And David fell—badly. He committed adultery with Bathsheba; he ordered her husband killed in battle; and he took a census of God's people when God said not to do it. When God wasn't enough for David, he ended up in sin and caused upheaval in the nation of Israel.

We can learn a powerful lesson on spiritual warfare from the account of David and the census.

*Satan rose up against Israel and caused David to take a census of
the people of Israel. So David said to Joab and the commanders*

of the army, "Take a census of all the people of Israel—from Beersheba in the south to Dan in the north—and bring me a report so I may know how many there are." But Joab replied, "May the LORD increase the number of his people a hundred times over! But why, my lord the king, do you want to do this? Are they not all your servants? Why must you cause Israel to sin?" But the king insisted that they take the census, so Joab traveled throughout all Israel to count the people.

(1 Chronicles 21:1–4 NLT)

There are three players in this story—Satan, David, and Joab.

"Satan rose up against Israel and caused David to take a census of the people." Can Satan actually *cause* you to do something? Can he force your hand? No, he can't. But he certainly can influence your thoughts and your mind. He can bombard you with the temptation to sin, attacking where he knows you are the weakest. Some translations use the word *incited* instead of caused. Satan definitely tempted or incited David to take a census of Israel. And David fell into sin.

"So David said to Joab and the commanders of the army, 'Take a census of all the people of Israel.'" David was walking in the flesh and in the pride of life. He wanted to know the exact count so he could boast about the large number of people under his rule. David was guilty of pride. Satan won this battle because he tempted David in his weakness, and David fell. He took his eyes off the Lord and placed it on his own earthly kingdom. This was not like the census that God ordered Moses to take, which was used to help subsidize the tabernacle. (See Exodus 30:12–16.) David knew that…and so did Joab.

Look at Joab's response: *"May the LORD increase the number of his people a hundred times over! But why, my lord the king, do you want to do this? Are they not all your servants? Why must you cause Israel to sin?"*

Joab spotted the reason behind David's command right away. He recognized David's false pride over the size of his kingdom. Joab was not a perfect man, but in this situation, he was walking closer to God than David was. Joab wanted to please God instead of his flesh. Joab had the right answer and wanted to obey God. David did not.

SPIRITUAL WARFARE TAKES DISCERNMENT

Spiritual warfare takes great discernment. If David had been seeking God in prayer, he wouldn't have fallen to temptation. If he had been singing God's praises as he did when he was a younger man, he would have been sensitive to the Holy Spirit, and 70,000 people wouldn't have paid the price for David's sin. (See 1 Chronicles 21:14.)

Spiritual warfare is real—and we have to understand how to be successful against it. Who was it that initiated this whole thing? Look again at the first verse: "*Satan rose up against Israel.*" Many people will laugh when we say that Satan tempted or incited someone to do something. That is to be expected of unbelievers because their eyes have been blinded to spiritual truth. But this biblical account in 1 Chronicles is a powerful testimony to Christians that Satan will attack you at your weakest point and tempt you to do the opposite of what God has spoken. Recognizing Satan's tactics will help you to avoid falling into the traps he lays for you.

Ask yourself again. Is God enough for you? God has to be enough.

THE LORD IS SUPREME

"*The LORD your God is supreme over all gods and over all powers. He is great and mighty, and he is to be obeyed. He does not show partiality, and he does not accept bribes*" (Deuteronomy 10:17 GNT). God is supreme over all rulers and over all powers. We acknowledge the fact that Satan has a kingdom, but it's a little "k" kingdom. God's kingdom is almighty. God's kingdom is supreme. God's kingdom holds all authority over everyone and everything.

David forgot the supremacy of almighty God. He made a decision to place his wishes over God's Word. That will always bring disaster. And it will limit our ability to walk in the power and spiritual freedom that God wants us to have.

Overcoming in spiritual battles is based upon our submission to God. The success of spiritual warfare is based upon our complete and utter submission to the King of Kings and Lord of Lords. Our success in spiritual warfare requires that we fight against the enemy of our soul—*God's way.*

God has to be enough for you to be successful in the spiritual realm. God wasn't enough for David's son, Solomon, either. What a sad thing. Eventually, Solomon's sin cost the Israelites their kingdom. God must be enough. You must take time to minister to almighty God. I grew spiritually, physically, mentally, emotionally, and financially when I learned to minister in love to God. To praise and hallow His name, to spend time with Him, and to acknowledge that it is all about the Father, Son, and Holy Spirit.

Let's go to prayer together today recognizing in faith that God will always be enough for us. Join us for prayer on Day 17 at www.pray21days.com or www.strategicrenewal.com/21days.

Day 18

The Power of Forgiveness

Jim Maxim

Bearing with one another and, if one has a complaint against
another, forgiving each other; as the Lord has forgiven you,
so you also must forgive.
—Colossians 3:13

Forgiveness helps to create the atmosphere that tears down strongholds and sets captives free. In God's kingdom, forgiveness delivers spiritual freedom and spiritual power. We need to understand the power of forgiveness if we are really going to step into the authority and victory that God has for us, to operate and live in forgiveness daily.

For you, O Lord, are good and forgiving, abounding in steadfast
love to all who call upon you. (Psalm 86:5)

Almighty God is full of mercy and forgiveness. He reveals His forgiveness towards us in His Word.

[God] does not deal with us according to our sins, nor repay us
according to our iniquities. For as high as the heavens are above
the earth, so great is his steadfast love toward those who fear him;

> **as far as the east is from the west**, *so far does he remove our*
> *transgressions from us.*   (Psalm 103:10–12)

> *He will again have compassion on us; he will tread our iniquities*
> *underfoot. You will cast all our sins* **into the depths of the sea**.
>   (Micah 7:19)

In the New Testament, we witness forgiveness in Jesus Christ—in both His actions and words. *"But if we walk in the light, as he is in the light, we have fellowship with one another, and the blood of Jesus his Son cleanses us from all sin"* (1 John 1:7). In the Lord's Prayer, Jesus says, *"And forgive us our debts, as we also have forgiven our debtors. And lead us not into temptation, but deliver us from the evil one"* (Matthew 6:12–13 NIV). You see, Jesus spoke about the importance of forgiveness *before* He asked the Father to *"deliver us from the evil one."* This is a spiritual principle. Jesus set up the spiritual order that forgiveness should come *before* deliverance. Since He set forgiveness first, we need to do the same.

Nothing revealed the depth of God's forgiveness more than Jesus enduring the cross for our sake. All the hurt and pain Jesus suffered on the cross—the betrayal, the scourging, the crown of thorns, the pounding of nails—before He descended into the depths of the earth to face the domain of darkness, and before He rose from the dead, Jesus *forgave*. Before completing His mission, Jesus had to say out loud to everyone who could hear Him: *"Father, forgive them for they do not know what they are doing."* (Luke 23:34 NIV). He had to say it out loud for our sake, too. *"Father, forgive them."*

By forgiving others, we are submitting to His will. The Lord's Prayer tells us, *"Your kingdom come, your will be done, on earth as it is in heaven"* (Matthew 6:10). In heaven, *everyone* submits to God. There is no dispute in heaven over who's the Ruler of the universe! Here on earth, we need to align our spirits completely with His. We don't want anything to come between us and almighty God—not our spirit, our attitude, or our thoughts. We want to be pure before Him. That has to include forgiveness.

Too many Christians fail to understand the power of forgiveness. Forgiveness allows us to *let it go in God*. It is the ability to no longer hold a grudge, no longer tell others what that person did to hurt you, no longer gossip about the offender. You might be asking, "But how can I forgive? How do I forgive if the hurt or betrayal has been so deep?" I understand your pain. Even better, Jesus understands your pain. You can call out to Him, "Jesus, please help me to forgive!" He will help you to rely on the power and the love of the Holy Spirit to forgive where it seems impossible.

When you first make the decision to forgive someone, you might still feel some of the hurt or anger. God says that He blots out our sins, and He no longer remembers them. "*I, I am he who blots out your transgressions for my own sake, and I will not remember your sins*" (Isaiah 43:25). But it's not always so easy for us.

As humans, it may be hard to forget the offenses against us, but the only way we will gain complete freedom in Christ is when we forgive others the way God wants us to. If we want to go on with God, if we want to grow closer to Him, we must forgive those who have offended us. If we are in the captivity of unforgiveness, we can't be the people God wants us to be. The good news is that we have the power of the Holy Spirit within to help us to forgive. God loves us so much that He won't let us go on with our sin of unforgiveness.

So today, we're asking God to forgive us, and we are forgiving those who have offended or hurt us. Can you think of someone who has offended you? Remember, the Lord's Prayer says, "Father, forgive *us* as we forgive *them*." It could be your spouse, children, parents, siblings, extended family, friends old and new, pastors or people in the church who have offended you. Learn to forgive. Learn to keep a clean heart before God and to forgive those who have hurt you. This may not mean returning to a close relationship, but you can make the conscious and deliberate decision to release them and be set free!

Today, I pray that the presence of God falls upon you so mightily that you will receive His power to forgive the people who hurt you, whose arrows pierced you deeply. Satan uses other people's offenses like fiery darts to penetrate your heart and try to destroy your faith. But you will receive the power of the Holy Spirit to quench those arrows when you say what Jesus said, *"Father, forgive them…"* I pray to God that today your eyes are open to the power of forgiveness. I pray that under the anointing of the Holy Spirit of God, you would forgive all those who have offended you. Say the following prayer with me now:

Father, in the name of Jesus Christ, I ask that You look deep into my soul. Father, in every aspect of my mind, my heart, my soul, my spirit, I want You to cleanse me and forgive me. Father, as I open myself up to You, I pray that the Holy Spirit would bring to my mind anything that I have done, Lord, that has offended You. I want to be totally and completely free.

Father, You see the hurts placed in my heart by certain people. You see how they have wounded me deeply. Father, just as Jesus did on the cross, I forgive [add their names]. As I speak these names out loud today, I ask You to forgive me for holding unforgiveness or even hatred against these offenders. Lord, forgive me for any bitterness I have held against anyone. I want to be right before You, Father. Help me to walk in forgiveness.

Now, let's go to God together in prayer for loved ones who we know are held captive in the stronghold of unforgiveness or who need our prayers for other deliverance. Join us for prayer on Day 18 at www.pray21days.com or www.strategicrenewal.com/21days.

A Change of Course

Jim Maxim

Have mercy on those who doubt;
save others by snatching them out of the fire.
—Jude 1:22–23

I've met so many people who think that, because of their monetary success and affluent lifestyle, they don't need God. They think that only those with *problems* need Christianity, that they have all they need to live a good life and contribute to society apart from bowing their knee to Jesus Christ.

The Bible says something very different. *"The fool says in his heart, 'There is no God'"* (Psalm 53:1). The most foolish thing you can do is reject God. The most intelligent thing you can ever do in the entire universe is to acknowledge almighty God. *"The fear [reverence] of the LORD is the beginning of wisdom"* (Proverbs 9:10).

God has called me to share the good news of salvation in Jesus Christ wherever I go. I feel compelled by His Spirit to *snatch people out of the fire.* One of the greatest things that God has allowed me to do in the years I have served Him is to pray this prayer every day.

"Father, please use me today to make faith come alive in somebody's heart somewhere. Please God, give me the ability to describe You to somebody else." It is a spiritual war I can wage in the heavenlies for someone's soul.

A CHANGE OF COURSE

Not long ago, I was playing golf in a foursome. My golf cart partner was a young guy, about thirty-five years old. I had never met him before, and he was excited to talk to me about growing his business. I am a Christian who happens to be successful in business, so he wanted to pick my brain as we traveled the course.

Immediately, I sensed in my spirit that God was opening the doors to share the love of Christ with him. The Holy Spirit spoke to my heart to do something I had never done before. I pulled a hundred-dollar bill out of my pocket, and I handed it to him.

"What does it say on this bill?" I asked him.

"What do you mean?" he answered.

"Well, you want to be successful, right? You want to make lots of these, right?"

"Yes, I do."

"Then, let's just see what it says on this bill."

"It says, 'In God We Trust,'" he answered.

"Ever ask yourself what that means?"

"Not really," was his puzzled reply.

"The U.S. government, the most powerful in the world, has printed on our money—the thing we covet the most—a reminder. Let me tell you how this happened. At the height of the Cold War, the Soviet Union was spreading atheism and communism throughout the world, declaring that the state was their god and would supply all of their needs. In response, some of the leaders in Washington, D.C., asked God how the United States could honor Him instead. The result was 'In God We Trust' printed on all U.S. currency, to 'serve as a constant reminder that the nation's political and economic fortunes were tied to its spiritual faith.'[7]

"You can still look at your money today. It says, *In God We Trust*. But who is this God who sacrificed His own Son? We are in a spiritual fight. He is a God we can trust to deliver us." Then I asked him, "Have you ever had these thoughts, 'I don't trust God. I don't need Him at all; I'd rather do it myself. I don't want to look like a weak Christian.'"

"Yes, a little bit," he answered.

"Let me ask you another question. Have you ever asked why Jesus Christ died on that tree for you? Have you ever asked why He sacrificed Himself for you?

"I can tell you one thing, my friend," I confided. "Yes, I made God my partner in business. But I made Him my Lord, my King, and my Savior first. Why wouldn't I want Jesus Christ to cleanse me and save me from my sin? I know what it is like for Him to cleanse me from drugs and alcohol, from living an upside-down life."

He looked at me quietly as I asked him, "Would you like to accept Jesus Christ as your Lord and Savior today on this golf course? Would you like to end this rat race once and for all and place Jesus Christ first in your life?"

We were out West at the time, and I live on the East Coast. I said to him, "I will probably never see you again after today. But I want

---

7. "Historical Highlights: The Legislation Placing 'In God We Trust' on National Currency," July 11, 1955, history.house.gov; search: In God We Trust.

you to know that the greatest thing you will ever do is to acknowledge that almighty God is your Father and that Jesus Christ is the Savior of mankind. But you have to acknowledge Him. You have to ask Him to forgive you."

This entire encounter happened in about fifteen minutes. We were sitting in our golf cart, waiting for the foursome in front of us to keep moving. I had two other friends sitting in a golf cart close by who were already believers, and, of course, they were praying.

That young man looked me squarely in the eyes and said, "Yes, I want to ask Christ into my life."

"Great. Let's pray."

"Jesus, forgive me," he prayed out loud. "Jesus, cleanse me. Jesus, I'm sorry I never recognized You. I'm sorry I never trusted You. Come into my life. Please God, I see that in my own stubbornness, I rejected You. But I ask You to forgive me. God cleanse me; come into my life and set me free."

Right there on that crowded golf course, Jesus Christ saved this young man. I believe it was because somebody was interceding for him. I don't know who, but Jesus Christ heard the cries of someone on his behalf. I am just so thankful that I was the one to see him surrender his life and enter the kingdom of God! I emailed him a few days later and sent him one of my books.

I don't know who was praying for that young man, but I know one thing: God answered those prayers. Prayer can be the conduit to bring a person to the end of themselves and that's where the power of the cross comes in. That is where someone will be willing to recognize their utter and complete dependence on Jesus.

There is only one person who can get us into heaven. There is only one name that can set someone free. That person, that name, is Jesus. He shed His atoning blood for us so that we will be completely free.

Let's go to God and pray for the people you know who need to surrender their life to Jesus. Join us for prayer on Day 19 at www.pray21days.com or www.strategicrenewal.com/21days.

Day 20

Reset the Spiritual Climate

Jim Maxim

I will extol you, my God and King,
and bless your name forever and ever.
—Psalm 145:1

When you face a spiritual battle, when you are unsure of what to do, you need to reset the spiritual climate. We have already covered many ways that you can do it—spending time worshipping God, taking up the powerful weapons of your warfare, holding up the truth of God's Word, and praying without ceasing. These divine tools set the spiritual atmosphere for your faith to grow and can reset the atmosphere when a spiritual battle looms.

My encouragement to believers in the middle of the battle is threefold:

1. Do not be afraid. Satan will always attack with fear, but we have been told, *"Fear not, for I am with you"* (Isaiah 41:10 NKJV).

2. Stand firm…*on your knees.* This doesn't mean sucking it up. It is not done in your own strength. We can fight Satan best

by holding up the shield of faith and the Word of God over everyone in our prayers.

3.   Believe in the love and goodness of God toward you.

Learning how to pull down strongholds requires learning how to go deeper with God and how to be a soldier of the cross. Facing the demonic activity that has our loved ones in the stronghold of hell is not a game. It's not made up, like some kind of weird, supernatural movie. Becoming a true soldier of the cross gives you such an anointing in your life that Satan flees from you and those you are praying for. *"Submit yourselves therefore to God. Resist the devil, and he will flee from you"* (James 4:7). This verse in the Greek literally means that Satan will run from you in terror! The enemy has to run when the focus is on God.

Resisting something takes work; it takes energy. In physical exercise, resistance training builds strong muscles. The same is true for spiritual warfare—resistance builds strength. Nothing good comes cheap. Most people aren't willing to pay the price. You have to practice changing the spiritual atmosphere. Submit to God and resist the devil; God will show you how. He'll open up your spiritual eyes. Stand in faith and push back against the enemy in the power of the Holy Spirit, refusing to accept the lies Satan plants in your mind. Become a soldier of the cross, a true believer in Jesus Christ. Walking in Christ's victory is our destiny.

Learning how to destroy strongholds requires understanding just what God has done for you. I never want to forget the day that Jesus Christ picked me up and washed me in His blood. I never want to forget the day that Jesus took authority over Satan in my life and delivered me from the domain of darkness.

Today, I would like to read God's Word with you. Read it out loud as you acknowledge His Kingdom, His power, and His love for us. How good, perfect, compassionate, and kind God is to us! Let's read Psalm 145:1–14 together.

I will extol you, my God and King, and bless your name forever and ever. Every day I will bless you and praise your name forever and ever. Great is the LORD, and greatly to be praised, and his greatness is unsearchable.

One generation shall commend your works to another, and shall declare your mighty acts. On the glorious splendor of your majesty, and on your wondrous works, I will meditate. They shall speak of the might of your awesome deeds, and I will declare your greatness. They shall pour forth the fame of your abundant goodness and shall sing aloud of your righteousness.

The LORD is gracious and merciful, slow to anger and abounding in steadfast love. The LORD is good to all, and his mercy is over all that he has made.

All your works shall give thanks to you, O LORD, and all your saints shall bless you! They shall speak of the glory of your kingdom and tell of your power, to make known to the children of man your mighty deeds, and the glorious splendor of your kingdom. Your kingdom is an everlasting kingdom, and your dominion endures throughout all generations.

[The LORD is faithful in all his words and kind in all his works.] The LORD upholds all who are falling and raises up all who are bowed down.

Let's go before God and do what these verses say to do right now. Let's enter into His presence and acknowledge His power, His holiness, His love, and His supremacy over us, our loved ones and all of the universe. Join us for prayer on Day 20 at www.pray21days.com or www.strategicrenewal.com/21days.

Day 21

The Secret of It All

Jim Maxim

Jesus answered him, "If anyone loves me, he will keep my word,
and my Father will love him,
and we will come to him and make our home with him."
—John 14:23

Let's pretend for a moment that you are with your loved ones, and you need to tell them the news the doctor just told you—you're going to die in the next twenty-four hours. Relax, I know that's a little strong! But this is an important lesson for us from God's Word.

Can you imagine the emotions you would feel and the state of mind that you and your loved ones would be in? What would your last words be to those you loved? Do you think those words would have a greater impact than any other conversation you ever had with them? I have walked with God for over five decades, and if I had the chance to speak with you on my last day on earth, this is what I would leave with you: Jesus's last words to His disciples.

Go with me to the book of Acts to read Jesus's final words on earth. Shut off the world around you on this twenty-first day of our journey together and focus your entire being—body, mind, and spirit—on what Jesus Christ said just before He ascended into heaven.

> [Jesus] *presented himself alive to them after his suffering by many proofs, appearing to them during forty days and speaking about the kingdom of God. And while staying with them he* **ordered them not to depart from Jerusalem, but to wait for the promise of the Father,** *which, he said,* "*you heard from me; for John bap-* **tized with water, but you will be baptized with the Holy Spirit not many days from now…You will receive power when the Holy Spirit has come upon you,** *and you will be my witnesses in Jerusalem and in all Judea and Samaria, and to the end of the earth.*" *And when he had said these things, as they were looking on, he was lifted up, and a cloud took him out of their sight.*
>
> (Acts 1:3–5, 8–9)

Jesus's last words on earth were clear. The Bible says He *ordered* His closest friends and family *not to do anything* until they *waited* upon Him and *received* from Him the power and help that only He and the Father could give—the Holy Spirit. Jesus had been preparing His disciples for a divine Helper. *"But I tell you the truth: it is to your advantage that I am leaving; for if I do not leave, the Helper will not come to you; but if I go, I will send Him to you"* (John 16:7 NASB). Jesus was saying, "I have nearly finished what My Father asked Me to do. It's time for Me to go. But you'll be glad because I am going to send you someone else, a divine Helper."

THE HOLY SPIRIT WITHIN US

Most Christians don't have a deep understanding of the Holy Spirit's role in the believer's life. Jesus declared that the Holy Spirit would be with us forever, *dwelling* with us and in us.

*I will ask the Father, and he will give you another Helper, to be with you **forever**, even the Spirit of truth, whom the world cannot receive, because it neither sees him nor knows him. You know him, **for he dwells with you and will be in you.***

(John 14:16–17)

Here we see the mystery of the Trinity—Father, Son, and Holy Spirit. God the Father sent Jesus Christ, His only Son, to die for you and me. Jesus obeyed His Father and willingly gave His life for our salvation. Then, Jesus's last words on earth were an order to His followers: Don't do anything until you wait for the Holy Spirit that We are sending to you. He will come upon you in power and dwell *with you and in you forever.*

But when the Helper comes, whom I will send to you from the Father, the Spirit of truth, who proceeds from the Father, he will bear witness about me.　　　　　(John 15:26)

Jesus also said, *"If anyone loves me, he will keep my word, and my Father will love him, and we will come to him and make our home with him"* (John 14:23). Who is the *"we"* who will make their home with us? These verses from John 15:26 and John 14:23 tell us it is the Father, the Son, and the Holy Spirit who will make Their home with us, who will dwell with us forever.

The Holy Spirit, the third Person of the Godhead, makes it possible for us to live the Christian life. He indwells us as our advocate, teacher, comforter, guide into truth, and revealer of the secrets of God.

*But the Helper, the Holy Spirit, whom the Father will send in my name, he will **teach you all things**.*　　　　　(John 14:26)

> *For **his Spirit searches out everything and shows us God's deep secrets**...We have received God's Spirit (not the world's spirit), so we can know the wonderful things God has freely given us.*
> (1 Corinthians 2:10, 12 NLT)

> *When the Spirit of truth comes, he will **guide you into all the truth**.*   (John 16:13)

A FRESH FILLING DAILY

The Holy Spirit renews us daily. I need to be filled fresh each and every day. As I praise and magnify the Father, Son, and Holy Spirit, I receive new strength for the day ahead of me. I need to be in Their holy presence every single day because I *leak*. I need to be filled fresh every day with God's love, power, and holy word to me for the day ahead. I *put on my armor* fresh for the fight of faith that I know is coming against me each day.

To be a victorious follower of Jesus in all of life, fellowship with the Father, Jesus, and the Holy Spirit needs to happen every day. And it happens best in your secret place. Jesus told us, "*When you pray, go into your room and shut the door and pray to your Father who is in secret. And your Father who sees in secret will reward you*" (Matthew 6:6).

It is the greatest privilege in the universe for a Christian—for me, for you—to have access to the living God. Nothing in this world can remotely compare to the privilege of walking into the holy of holies, spending time with my Father every day, bowing my heart and mind to Him, and thanking Him for the privilege of being His child because of Jesus's sacrifice. Here in the secret place, I can realign my spirit with God's Spirit. The greatest privilege we have, after salvation, is to be in the presence of the Father, Son, and Holy Spirit.

My brothers and sisters, please enter *the secret place* as Jesus described it. My heart's desire is for you to understand how vital it is to wait upon and walk in deep fellowship with God. It's here that God, through the Holy Spirit, will come upon you and demolish every stronghold that Satan has tried to build against you or your loved ones. It's here in the secret place that you will learn *the true secret* to it all—spending time with the Creator of the universe, loving and worshipping Him, confessing His power, His holiness, His omnipotence, His excellence. By getting lost in His presence, you will find the true power of the Holy Spirit. Your life will change forever. The Holy Spirit will give you wisdom, knowledge, and understanding for all you face in life. He will awaken your mind and quicken your spirit. He will help you to become the person that you truly want to be for God's glory.

OUT OF YOUR INNERMOST BEING

The Holy Spirit is the life and power within us. Jesus promised us that out of our innermost being would flow *"rivers of living water."*

> *Whoever believes in me, as the Scripture has said, "Out of his heart will flow rivers of living water." Now this he said **about the Spirit**, whom those who believed in him were to receive, for as yet the Spirit had not been given, because Jesus was not yet glorified.*
> (John 7:38–39)

There is no lack in the Holy Spirit's supply. There is no trickle in heaven of living waters. It's a God-sized flood! I want God to flow in me and on me and through me by His Holy Spirit! I know you want that, too.

Let's go before God today, asking Him to do just that—to flow on us, in us, and through us by His Holy Spirit. Let's spend this last day in prayer together ministering to the Father, the Son, and the Holy

Spirit. And may God bless you as you continue your journey with Him. Join us for prayer on Day 21 at www.pray21days.com or www.strategicrenewal.com/21days.

About the Authors

Over fifty years ago, Jim Maxim was at the lowest point of his life. As he lay at death's door, Jim's mother prayed for his soul. God answered her prayer, and Jim's life was claimed, redeemed, and transformed for Jesus Christ. The dramatic story of Jim's conversion is found in his book *Face to Face with God*.

After serving in the U.S. Marine Corps, Jim created multiple successful companies in the automotive industry. He serves God in prison ministries, as a church speaker, and as a board member of several ministries, including Hope Pregnancy Center, the Valley Forge Leadership Prayer Breakfast, and Strategic Renewal International (SRI).

In 2011, Jim and his wife, Cathy, founded Acts413 Ministries, where they evangelize, counsel, and minister in the name of Jesus all over the world. The highlight of Acts413 Ministries is to serve as a catalyst to mobilize the body of Christ to intercede for pastors, their families, and their churches. Jim prays and leads others in the power of intercessory prayer through God's Word. The desire of Jim and Cathy's hearts is to teach the vital key to growth as a child of the King—the glorious privilege of being in the presence of almighty God.

The Maxims have three sons, three daughters-in-law, and three grandchildren.

⌒

As a senior pastor for over two decades, Daniel Henderson brought prayer-based revitalization to numerous churches. Now, as the president of Strategic Renewal, he is dedicating his full-time efforts to help congregations across the country and world experience renewal.

Daniel is sought after for his expertise in leading corporate prayer. He has authored numerous books on biblical leadership and prayer, including *Old Paths, New Power* and *Transforming Prayer: How Everything Changes When You Seek God's Face.*